PETE ROSE'S
winning
baseball

PETE ROSE'S

winning
baseball

Pete Rose
with Bob Hertzel

Henry Regnery Company · Chicago

Library of Congress Cataloging in Publication Data

Rose, Pete, 1942-
  Winning baseball.

  Includes index.
  1. Baseball. I. Hertzel, Bob, 1941- joint author.
II. Title.
GV867.R55   1976   796.357'2   75-34476
ISBN 0-8092-8191-0
ISBN 0-8092-8102-3 pbk.

Published by Henry Regnery Company
180 North Michigan Avenue, Chicago, Illinois 60601
Manufactured in the United States of America
Library of Congress Catalog Card Number: 75-34476
International Standard Book Number: 0-8092-8191-0 (cloth)
                              0-8092-8102-3 (paper)

Published simultaneously in Canada by
Beaverbooks
953 Dillingham Road
Pickering, Ontario L1W 1Z7
Canada

contents

chapter one

everyone should be charlie hustle

The day I became something out of the ordinary was one spring day before I ever played a game in the major leagues. The year was 1963 and I was a brash kid up from the minor leagues trying to make it as a rookie second baseman with the Cincinnati Reds.

On this particular afternoon, we were playing the New York Yankees. The first time I went to bat I drew a base on balls and, as I had ever since I was nine years old, I ran to first base as hard as I could.

In the Yankee dugout—these were the days when the Yanks were still winning pennants—sat Mickey Mantle and Whitey Ford, a couple of guys who made their way into baseball's Hall of Fame. They saw me, an unknown rookie, going to first on a walk at full speed and they couldn't resist the temptation of riding me.

"Hey, you, Charlie Hustle," they started shouting. A few newspaper reporters were gathered there at the dugout (one of them Dick Young of the *New York Daily News),* and they heard Ford and Mantle teasing me and calling me Charlie Hustle. The next day in their newspapers, they used the name and it stuck.

Ever since, I have been Charlie Hustle and I consider it a good nickname. It also carries with it a large burden. As Charlie Hustle, I'm expected to live up to the name and forever be hustling.

Believe me, I live up to it and love every minute of it. The one thing people can never accuse me of is not hustling. With the nickname, it's hard not to give 100 percent all the time. Sure, people should expect every professional ball player to hustle, but it seems fans expect it more from me than anybody else.

YOU CAN'T BACK OFF. This was one of those plays where I could have gotten myself killed. Racing after a foul pop, I tripped over the pitcher's mound in the bullpen and crashed into the wall. Note in third picture I am still holding the ball in my glove. P.S. I played the next day. (Photos by Bob Free)

2

charlie hustle

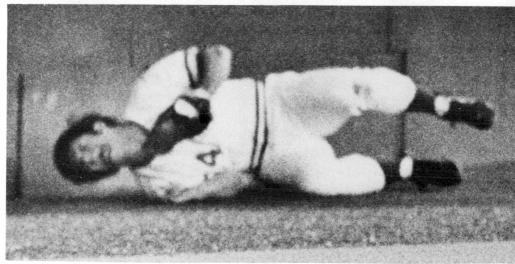

And to think, it all started because I ran to first base on a walk during an exhibition game. The Yankees thought that was really weird, but they shouldn't have. I picked it up from one of the men who once wore the Yankee pinstripes. I was nine years old and watching television with my father, who was a pretty good semipro player himself.

Enos Slaughter was playing that day and he drew a walk. Off he went as quickly as he could to first base. My father turned to me and said, "That's the way baseball ought to be played."

The idea stuck with me. He was, after all, right. It is the way to play baseball. It is, in fact, the way to do everything. Go through life hustling. That's my theory.

What, though, is hustling? I have my own idea about that. Hustling is just having fun. It's doing what you like to do. If you like to play baseball, you'll like playing it the right way and the right way is hustling.

I firmly believe you can win a lot of ball games with sheer hustle because you find yourself in the unexpected spot at just the right time. One play in particular stands out in my mind. We were playing in Atlanta Stadium on this day and I was in center field, with Alex Johnson—something less than a Gold Glove winner—in left.

Someone hit a high fly to left. A.J.—that's what we called Alex— went back to the wall. The baseball, however, was over the fence. A.J. leaped and swiped at the ball with his glove, trying to hit it back into the playing area.

And, that's just what he did. The ball came flying back into the field and guess who was there to catch it before it hit the ground? Charlie Hustle, that's who. Don't ask me why I was there on a long fly ball to left field that looked like a home run. I can't explain it other than to say there was nothing I could do in center field, so I hustled over. I was as surprised as anyone when the ball came to me. Instead of a home run or a double, the batter had nothing but an out to show for his long drive.

You hustle on defense and you hustle on offense and it leads to victories. I'll give you another example. We were playing the Cardinals in St. Louis a few years back and we weren't playing very well. We trailed, 6-0, with two out and none on in the eighth.

4

I hit a one-hopper right back to the pitcher, a sure out. But I still ran full speed to first base. Sure enough, the pitcher's throw was high and it pulled the first baseman off the base. I beat it out. If I had loafed down the line, cursing my bad luck, the first baseman would have had time to get back on the base. Running full speed prevented it.

It also prevented us from losing the game. We went on to score seven runs in the inning—starting with two out, none on, and a ground ball to the pitcher—and won the game, 7-6.

Hustle? It's the easiest thing in the world to do. In the big leagues, hustle usually means being in the right place at the right time. It means backing up a base. It means backing up your teammate. It means doing everything you can do to win a baseball game.

Determination. That's what hustle is. If you aren't determined, you can't hustle. You must be determined to get the most out of yourself and your ability. You must be determined to win.

You'd be surprised how many shortcomings can be overcome simply by hustle. I'm the perfect example of that. There are a lot of guys in the big leagues who have more ability than me—who run faster, throw harder, are stronger, are quicker. But I have gotten the most out of my ability.

My teammate, Joe Morgan, our All-Star second baseman, is the same way. He has pushed himself and studied himself so that he uses his ability to its fullest. This is most important. And it comes from hustle, which comes from determination.

DEVELOP A WINNING ATTITUDE

The decision to hustle is the first one a player should make before he decides to take up baseball. In fact, it is the first decision a person should make before he goes into anything. Selling insurance can be helped by hustle. So can digging a ditch or running a company.

The second thing that must come to a person, no matter what line he chooses, but especially in something like sports, is a winning attitude. And a winning attitude comes from confidence.

You have to believe in yourself and in your team if you are to succeed, and baseball is one of the hardest games in which to develop such an attitude. On the big league level, you go to spring training knowing that a successful season consists of 100 wins. But you also know that 100 wins means you will lose 62 games during the year. Sixty-two failures, at the minimum, stand before you—even if you are a winner!

Even though you know you are going to lose, you can never really accept it. Once you accept defeat, it becomes easy to lose. If defeat comes you face it and you take it, but you don't accept it. The next day, you must go out and try even harder to win and do everything in your power to bring about that victory.

Determination and hard work . . . belief in your team and yourself . . . that is what makes a winning attitude. To be even simpler, a winning attitude is nothing more than positive thinking, and I can't stress this enough.

If you don't think you can do something, there's no way you can do it. If you don't think you can hit, there's no way you can hit. If you don't think you can win, there's no way you can win.

You have to believe in what you have working for you, then you must use it. When you do that, you will be a winner. Believe me.

This belief in one's self, this mental aspect in the game of baseball, is so important. You see it all the time, especially when a player goes into a slump. I firmly believe that in most cases, a slump is 90 per cent mental and 10 per cent physical.

It may start with some tough luck in hitting. Then, maybe, comes a minor flaw in the swing. But after 0-for-8 or 0-for-13, a player begins to lose confidence in what he has done for his entire career. His attitude sours. He starts changing things and then he is dead.

It never ceases to amaze me. I see a guy who has had seven or eight very successful years in the big leagues go into a slump. Almost immediately, 10 guys are telling him what he's doing wrong and, more amazing, he listens and changes things.

Before you know it, he's lost confidence in all the things that worked for him before. He's trying new things in which he really has no confidence—and he has lost that belief in himself. He still has determination and he still may be hustling, but his winning attitude is shot.

6

What he needs now is a psychiatrist rather than a batting coach. When this happens, you'll see the batting coach try to get him back to his old successful ways. And you'll see the batting coach praying that he gets a couple of lucky hits—broken-bat bloops or seeing-eye ground balls—so his belief in himself will return.

AN INDIVIDUAL GAME

Baseball, you see, is unlike all other sports in one respect. It is a team game that is based on individual success. Combine all the individual successes, add in the teamwork that is so necessary in such things as bunting and double plays, and that is how you come up with your winners.

Take hitting, for example. Ted Williams, who is one of the all-time great hitters, has always said hitting is the hardest individual thing there is in sports. He's right. He's right because you are alone. No one is helping you. It is you against the pitcher.

In football, you are running for a touchdown while people block for you. In basketball, you drive for the basket and your teammates set picks for you. You get help.

Tennis and golf are individual sports, but remember, the crowd is working for you there. The fans aren't allowed to shout or cheer while you are performing. You are allowed to concentrate.

In baseball, though, the crowd may be booing you, the other bench riding you, and the catcher talking to you. I've had that happen many times. One time in particular stands out. We were playing the Philadelphia Phillies and Gene Mauch was managing them then. I had been on a tear and they just couldn't seem to get me out with anything.

When I came up to the plate, Mike Ryan, the Phils' catcher, said to me: "Pete, Mauch told me to tell you what pitch is coming."

And darn if he didn't do just that. Pitch after pitch, he told me what was coming and I just wouldn't believe him. I was 0-for-4 in the ninth inning when I came up with the game on the line.

"Okay, here comes a curve," said Ryan.

"Well, he hasn't lied to me all game, I don't guess he will now," I thought to myself.

I waited for the curve, got it, and hit it out of the park to win the game. Next day, when I came to the plate for the first time, Ryan looked up at me and said: "Mauch told me to tell you to go jump in the lake."

See what I mean about distractions? You are alone against the pitcher and eight fielders . . . not particularly good odds. That is why you have to do something to help the odds.

And that something is hustle and belief in yourself. If you do that, you are way ahead of the game.

CONDITIONING AND DIET

I'm going to surprise you here. Baseball is not a strenuously physical game. To play baseball, you do not have to be in as good shape as to play basketball, for example, or football. In basketball, you are forever running. In football, you are testing your strength.

In baseball, how often is it that you are asked to run out a triple . . . once a week?

But don't get me wrong. I believe you must be in condition to play at your best. You must spend the early part of the year—spring training in professional baseball—running a great deal to get your legs in shape. You don't have to be a miler, but you do need to be able to go through the season at full speed without injuries such as pulled muscles.

There is an exception to the rule. A pitcher must have his legs in the best shape possible. I've never pitched, but I know. Oh, how I know. I've thrown batting practice in spring training and, believe me, 20 minutes of throwing batting practice and you're dizzy. You have to be in top condition to pitch.

Usually a player learns what he needs to get into shape, although on the Little League or high school level, the coach probably has the best idea. He will prescribe how much running he thinks is right and how many calisthenics should be done.

Stretching exercises are good, as they prevent pulled muscles but, once again, there are some individuals who need less of this than others. I don't get pulled muscles so I need fewer stretching exercises than Joe Morgan, who does come up with pulls.

I also am not a great believer in weights or isometric exercises. The strength in baseball isn't nearly as important as flexibility. If you develop your muscles to too great an extent, it restricts your movement. And restricted movement hinders the swing and the throwing motion.

I do believe in doing any exercises that will increase a player's speed. Speed is the greatest physical asset there is in baseball. It is the only thing that helps both on offense and defense.

A talk with a track coach on how to develop speed might help a high school player, especially in his first year. All you have to do is watch one ball game and see how many men are out by a step, or see how many balls are one step out of a fielder's reach, and you understand why speed is so important.

There are areas where strength should be worked on. Your hands, wrists, and forearms are very important to hitting and throwing. Squeezing a hand grip or a little sponge-rubber ball in your spare time can help here. This can be done while you're watching a movie with your high school sweetheart, if that's where you care to do it.

The diet is something that is badly overlooked by many, especially in this day of the quickie hamburger, pizza pie, and milk shake.

I am a steak-and-salad man. That does two things. It gives me protein and it helps control my weight. I've seen guys literally eat themselves right out of the big leagues and that is a shame because it is much easier to control your diet than it is to hit a slider.

A good breakfast, a good steak, as few fried foods and sweets as possible . . . that is my recommendation.

chapter two

Thank you, Dad. I've said that many, many times over the years. And every time I've said it, I've meant it. My father is responsible for my becoming a switch-hitter and, as far as I'm concerned, that's been the most important thing in my baseball career.

Once again, I was nine years old when it happened. I was about to enter knothole baseball—Cincinnati's Little League. My father had decided that I was to become a switch-hitter. He had worked hard with me.

But he was worried that a coach of a knothole team might not like the idea and not let me switch-hit. So, my dad went to the coach.

"Look," he said, "I want you to promise me one thing. No matter what the situation—game-winning run on third base or anything—I want Pete to be able to bat left-handed against a right-handed

i'd rather switch
than fight

pitcher and right-handed against a left-handed pitcher."

"No problem," answered the coach, promising he'd allow me to switch-hit all the time.

That one little conversation turned into the biggest moment in my life. Ever since then, I've been dedicated to switch-hitting.

I am forever being asked by people if I'd advise a young player to learn to hit both ways. My answer is always the same. If a kid has the talent, I strongly recommend he give it a try. And, he should start young.

But I also go one step further when I make the suggestion. I tell him that if anyone is to become a successful switch-hitter, he'd better be dedicated and prepared to practice a lot.

I can't tell you how long I practiced hitting left-handed. I'm a natural right-handed hitter. Today, though, I believe I hit better the opposite way.

Why? A couple of reasons, and the first one is practice. To compensate for being a little slower left-handed and because I had to work so much harder at it, I practiced more from the left side.

The second reason is that there are more right-handed pitchers around. Hence, you will bat more left-handed.

If I figured it up, I would guess that over my life, I have spent three times as much time hitting left-handed as right-handed and it has paid off handsomely. It can for you, too, if you have the desire and determination—call it hustle, if you like—to spend hour upon hour practicing hitting both ways.

WHY SWITCH HIT?

The answer to this question comes not from the hitter, but from the pitcher. It is the pitcher who makes switch-hitting an advantage.

The pitches that most batters have trouble with today are the curve ball and the slider, especially when they are thrown from a sidearm or three-quarter delivery. A right-handed batter facing a right-handed pitcher who seems to be throwing from third base with that big sidearm motion has a tendency to bail out. He will step toward third base.

As a switch-hitter, you don't have this problem. The curve and the slider are always coming in to you. They are easier to see and easier to hit that way.

Believe me, switch-hitting would be of no value if 8 out of 10 pitchers threw screwballs. The screwball, you see, thrown by a right-hander like Mike Marshall of the Los Angeles Dodgers, breaks away from a left-handed hitter—much like a left-hander's curve.

It is tough for a switch-hitter to hit this pitch. But he doesn't have to worry about it much. Eight out of 10 pitchers don't throw screwballs.

However, 10 out of 10 pitchers throw curves and sliders and they are the toughest pitches to handle. Therefore, switch-hitting is an invaluable weapon if you can handle it.

The switch-hitter does one other thing. He puts a bit of a burden on the opposing manager in key points in a game. The manager feels he has to go to the bullpen. Should he come in with a left-hander or a right-hander? Does it make any difference? See what I mean?

THE GREAT SWITCH-HITTERS

It seems that today, more than ever, the big leagues are blessed with good switch-hitters. The St. Louis Cardinals have two of the best in Ted Simmons, their catcher, and outfielder Reggie Smith. Both combine average with power.

Baltimore has a good one in outfielder Ken Singleton. Philadelphia has my little buddy Larry Bowa at shortstop; my other little buddy, Bud Harrelson, hits from both sides for the Mets.

Probably the greatest switch-hitter of all time, of course, was the man who helped give me my nickname—Mickey Mantle. What a career he had. He played 18 years with the Yankees and hit .298 lifetime with 536 home runs and 1,509 runs batted in.

Until Mantle came along, the man considered the greatest switch-hitter of all time was Frankie Frisch, the old Fordham Flash, who played 19 years and hit for a .316 lifetime batting average.

Frisch amassed 2,880 hits, which is the all-time record for a switch-hitter and is one of the things I'm intent on breaking. I want to be known as the switch-hitter who got the most hits in his career. I have worked so hard that I feel this would be a fitting reward.

Already I own a few switch-hitting records. I had the most hits in a season, 230 in 1973 when I won my third batting title and was named the Most Valuable Player in the National League, and most singles in a season, 181, that same year.

Another switch-hitter of note was Maury Wills of the Dodgers, who stole 104 bases in 1962, a record that was broken in 1974 by Lou Brock of the St. Louis Cardinals. Wills, by the way, credits switch-hitting with bringing him to the major leagues.

He had banged around the minor leagues for nine years before he finally got his chance and he believes he never would have had the chance had not Bobby Bragan, his minor league manager, changed him into a switch-hitter.

So, you see, it's never too late if you have the ability and the desire. But still, the best way is to find out young if you can do it and then stick with it, no matter what.

13

chapter three

In 1941 Ted Williams hit .406 for the Boston Red Sox. Since then, no one has managed to hit .400 over a full season.

Nobody asked me, but I don't believe anyone ever will hit .400 again. Let me alter that statement somewhat. There could be a .400 hitter if the guy would go to bat only 350 or 400 times in a season.

That way, two or three really hot months would throw him over the top. But I see no way for a man who goes to the plate 600 times—like I do and like most regulars do—to hit .400.

One reason is that the pitching today is just too good. Another reason is that the relief pitching is too good. And the third reason is that the pressure is just too much to take. I don't mean the pressure from the press or the public. That can be handled.

What I mean is the pressure of knowing that every day, day in and

hitting: the basics

day out, you have to get two hits. That's what it would take to hit .400. One hit a day doesn't do it. Two hits one day and one the next doesn't do it. I don't care how lucky you are, how good you are, what color you are, you just can't get two hits every day.

What I'm saying is something I alluded to earlier. Hitting is anything but easy. It's hard, the hardest thing there is to do in sports.

Check out the major leagues. These are the guys who are supposed to be the best at what they do. What's a good average in major league baseball? I'll tell you. A good average is .300.

Now, think about .300 for a moment. What does that mean? That means for every 10 times to the plate, a batter hits safely three times. To put it a different way, it means for every 10 times to the plate, he is out seven times.

Seven out of 10 times up you fail and you are considered good, one of the best. Try that in golf, hitting the fairway with just three of 10 drives. Or try it in tennis, getting just three of 10 serves in. You're not doing so well in those sports, are you?

Let's take a hard look at the big leagues for a moment. There is not one player in the game today with a lifetime batting average near .333. That is one out of three successes or two out of three failures. No one is near it.

Ty Cobb is considered the greatest average hitter in the game. For his lifetime, he hit .367, a mark that no one really approaches. This is utterly spectacular, a .367 average accumulated over 24 seasons. If you hit that high one year today, you are assured the batting title.

In 1973 I hit .338 and won the batting title easily. In 24 years, Ty Cobb hit that "low" just six times, topping .338 in 18 seasons.

Yes, the man had to be a super hitter. But, let me tell you, no one can convince me that if he had come into the league in 1963 like I did and played 12 years, that he would have a .367 lifetime average. I just can't believe that.

I have no idea what he'd hit. If I had to guess, I would say his lifetime average would be around .315 or .320, maybe a bit higher.

What then is the difference between hitting today and hitting in the 1920s when Ty Cobb and Babe Ruth were around? I would say the big difference between hitters today and hitters then is relief pitching.

Managers nowadays tell their starting pitcher to pitch as hard as he can for as long as he can. Then, when the starter gets tired, he brings in a relief pitcher earning $100,000 a year to face two batters. And he tells that $100,000-a-year guy not to worry because he can bring in a guy making $50,000 to pitch to one hitter.

You are, in effect, always facing a fresh pitcher. That, you had better believe, hurts batting averages. It also hurts egos.

There are other factors that make hitting in the big leagues today tougher than ever before. One factor is that the season starts earlier and earlier, meaning more cold weather. And no one wants to hit in cold weather. Some hitters can't get loose. You don't take a lot of batting practice, mainly because if you take one on the hands, it stings for two days.

Television hasn't helped the hitter any, either. We are starting so many games to benefit television or Saturday night crowds that it is hurting averages. We play at 4 PM and 5:30 PM and if the sun is shining, you just can't see the ball right because of the glare.

You have to play games, too, in the Astrodome, something Ty Cobb never had to contend with. Seeing the baseball is hard in the dome and it hurts the average.

And AstroTurf hurts hitting. That may be hard to believe, as fast as the artificial surface is, but it does. The infielders play so deep on AstroTurf that no matter how fast you run, the ball gets to the fielder faster and he can throw you out. And bunting on artificial turf is tougher so you can almost throw that out as an offensive weapon.

IT'S YOUR CHOICE

Now that I have thoroughly discouraged you about the art of hitting, let me tell you that you can become a good hitter. Rogers Hornsby, probably the greatest right-handed hitter of all time, once said that great hitters are made and not born.

I can buy that. Certainly you must have some natural things going for you. Most important, you must like the game of baseball and you must have the desire and dedication to work at the game.

You also have to have good reflexes and eyesight, but remember this: Everyone with good reflexes or good eyesight is not a good hitter.

A good hitter does a little thinking, a little playing, and a lot of practicing. Practice is the key. Once you get everything straight in your mind, you must go out and practice and practice and practice.

Sometime along the way, you are going to have to make one vital decision. What kind of hitter are you going to be? Are you going to switch-hit or are you going to stick with your natural way of hitting? It's your choice with my advice being switch-hit if possible.

Maybe more important, are you going to be a power hitter or not? This decision will influence almost everything about you as a hitter and it is an individual decision.

A long time ago, I made the decision that I was going to be a singles hitter. I also made up my mind that I was going to be the first singles hitter to earn $100,000 a year. I made it. I made it for other people who want to go for average rather than home runs. I wanted to show them that money can be made hitting singles.

In 1974 Ralph Garr of the Braves, who went on to win the batting championship, called me aside one day.

"Pete, I just want to thank you," Ralph said. "You're the guy who made it possible for a guy like me to make big money. You set all the standards."

That made me feel good. I probably could have been a home run hitter, especially if I had stayed right-handed from the time I was a kid. I'm not small, 200 pounds, and in batting practice, I can hit the ball as far as anyone.

But I developed my own individual way of hitting. I developed a line-drive type swing and I hit the ball where it's pitched.

The same decision is one you'll have to wrestle with. Some of it will have to do with the type of team you're on. If you are the only player with any power, you may have to go for power. If there are three other strong men, you may go for the hits.

By playing every day and learning about yourself and your abilities, you'll learn exactly what kind of hitter you should be.

The guy who comes to mind when I think about this is Eddie Brinkman, the shortstop with the New York Yankees. Eddie and I grew up together. We played on the same knothole teams and we played in high school with each other.

In high school, he was a Babe Ruth. I mean he was down on the end of the bat hitting home runs for Western Hills High School, the big slugger.

But he learned. Most of your professional players hit .480 or .500 and hit home runs when they were in high school. Then they get into the big time and someone says to them, "Kid, you won't make it hitting home runs."

The decision is made for them. Today, Eddie Brinkman chokes up eight inches on the bat and could care less whether he ever hits another ball out of the park.

As I said, this decision will be based on you as an individual. If you are a 250-pound giant, take a big bat at the bottom and swing for the fences. If you are a 175-pound shortstop who finds the fences a bit too distant, learn to slap the ball around.

Most of my theories are for the guy who tries to hit for average. But never let it be said they are for a man who hits the ball weakly. The one thing I believe in is hitting the ball hard.

That makes sure the outfielders can't play shallow, thereby taking hitting area away from you.

SELECTING A BAT

We come now to the first rule of hitting: *Be comfortable.* It is as simple as that. And your comfort begins with the selection of the bat you will use.

This may be the most important thing you do when it comes to becoming a good hitter. It's like a doctor who is going to operate on someone. He has to have the right scalpel. The same thing goes for the guy trying to hit. He has to have the right bat.

And the right bat is the one that fits your hands and feels good to you. Because Pete Rose is your favorite player is no reason to use a Pete Rose model bat. After all, that bat was picked by me because it felt comfortable to me. I wasn't even thinking about you.

You see so many guys who don't hit because they don't have the right bat. Maybe they have a bat that is too heavy and they are late swinging or maybe the bat is too light and they are out front, swinging before the ball gets to them.

Always remember this, hit to your qualifications. If you are a 250-pounder, take a big bat and swing it. If you can't handle that kind of bat, consider a lighter one.

I myself am a picky hitter. I like a wide-grained bat. I cannot hit without using pine tar, a sticky substance that helps your grip on the bat. When I go to take extra batting practice in spring training, I have to have the pine tar with me. This is probably a mental thing with me, but it has to do with feeling comfortable. I don't feel comfortable without pine tar.

My bat is what you'd call medium. It weighs about 34½ ounces

PINE TAR. It's important to feel comfortable at the plate. I don't feel comfortable without pine tar, a sticky substance that gives you a better grip on the bat. Here I apply pine tar before going up to hit. (Photo by Fred Straub)

and is 36 inches long. Dick Allen, they say, used the heaviest bat in the big leagues, about 40 ounces. Once again, this is a matter of individual taste and physical assets.

If a bat is too light, I absolutely refuse to use it. That doesn't mean if it weighs less than 34 ounces. That means if it "feels" too light. I'd rather a bat be a little heavy than too light. I will go ahead with a bat that feels a bit heavy, but never with one that's too light.

I use a skinny-handled bat. Once again, you will have to decide whether you want a skinny-handled bat or one with a fat handle. The thin-handled bat makes it easier to pull the ball.

Most of the guys who use a thick-handled bat choke up and punch at the ball. They don't hit with power. They don't pull the ball. They hold the bat three or four inches from the bottom and push at the ball.

I don't believe in pulling the ball as a rule but I do believe in having some power. You know, keep those outfielders honest.

Most power hitters use the skinny-handled bat. They can flip it faster, get more whip and more bat speed, and therefore more power.

I don't change bats during the season. I have found the model I like and I stick with it. It's called an S-222. You can come by my home in Cincinnati and check out my All-Star bats for the past nine years. They are all the same. The only difference is that at one time, I used an S-2 instead of an S-222. The S-222 has a bit bigger handle, but that is the only difference.

A lot of players change bats because they think they're getting tired and need a lighter bat. But I believe you won't get tired if you get enough sleep and eat the right food.

Above all else, though, the one rule to remember in selecting a bat is to pick one with which you are comfortable.

GETTING A GRIP

Now that you have a comfortable bat, a tool to work with, so to speak, we now must figure out how to use that tool. And the first thing we come to is how to hold the bat.

GRIPPING THE BAT. The bat should lie down in the fingers, not way back in the palm of the hand. The knuckles of one hand are aligned with the second joint of the fingers of the other hand. Grip the bat firmly but don't squeeze sawdust out of it. Get yourself the right grip because the hands are the most important part of hitting. (Photos by Fred Straub)

There are many different grips you can use. You can take the bat and squeeze the daylights out of it. I don't recommend this because it restricts your freedom of motion and, therefore, restricts your swing.

You can hold the bat lightly. This is not a particularly good idea if you keep the grip that way while you swing.

The best way to hold the bat is firmly, with the hands together, right hand on top if you are batting right-handed and left on top if left-handed. Your hands are relaxed, but firm, and as the swing starts, you tighten on the bat so that you get all of your power.

Once again, I can't say what is right for you. It is a matter of comfort. If holding the bat balanced on one finger feels comfortable to you—and you can hit like that—go ahead. The more power to you.

I have found that the bat lies across my hand at the base of my fingers. It is this area that becomes calloused from swinging. Callouses are good for you as a hitter. I'll work hard all spring getting blisters and then callouses to toughen the hand so I can go through the season without getting sore hands.

I hold the bat down at the end. You may want to choke up. If you are a real power hitter, you may want your bottom finger to actually extend over the knob at the end of the bat. Once again, comfort and individual taste.

As I hold the bat, the knuckles of my top hand are aligned with the large joint in the fingers of my bottom hand. That gives me the most freedom of movement and bat control.

The more the knuckles rotate toward each other, the more the tendency to pull the ball and, once again, I don't believe in being strictly a pull hitter.

One thing about the grip is for certain. Find the one that fits you best and stay with it. My theory of hitting is that you hit with the hands and the grip is what puts the hands in contact with the bat. The importance of the grip cannot be slighted.

TAKING YOUR STANCE

We go back to rule Number 1 about hitting. Be comfortable when you pick a stance. There is no right stance, just as there is no wrong stance. Whatever way you feel best is the way you should set yourself in the batter's box.

Over the years, there have been some radical stances. Stan Musial used to stand way back in the box, feet close together, his body crouched and turned so that he looked like he was peeking over his shoulder at the pitcher. But he got the most out of his stance. He stayed on the ball longer than most and when he came out of that coil, he came out sharply and smoothly.

A lot of guys with radical stances don't get all they should out of their stance. They get tied up. Tito Fuentes of San Diego, who, batting left-handed, stands almost with his back to the pitcher, is one such player who gets tied up.

My stance is somewhat radical since I take a deep crouch. My feet are a little bit farther apart than the average spread, about shoulder-width apart or a little farther. I take a small stride and try to keep my weight on my back foot.

I believe keeping the weight back until the last possible moment is very important. It's the reason why I'm seldom fooled by a pitch and why I'm a good change-up hitter.

My stride is a short one, about six inches. A guy who takes a big stride is going to be subject to the change-up or off-speed curve ball. You can catch him out on his front foot, the wrong foot to hit off. Unless you're a Henry Aaron, you don't want to be fooled too often.

That's why I recommend keeping the weight back in the stance and the feet spread wide, cutting down on the stride.

Your hands must be kept back. This is basic. About eight inches from the body is plenty. But once again, be comfortable. My hands, for example, start right about next to my ear. That's comfortable for me.

Once you find your stance, stick with it. I don't recommend changing the stance and I certainly would never ask a hitter to change his stance unless it was the cause of some basic flaw in his swing.

If things start going wrong, don't look toward your stance for the answer. If it was successful before, something else must be the trouble. There are four things I would recommend you change when you aren't swinging the bat well: Pick up a lighter bat or a heavier one. Move up on the plate or move back.

If you are swinging too hard, take a heavier bat. That will cut down on your swing. If you aren't swinging hard enough, go to a lighter bat. Maybe the curve ball is getting to you. Move back. Or maybe you're not getting to the curve. Better move up. Whatever you do, don't mess with the stance.

Where should you stand in the box? Once again, you will have to discover the ideal spot yourself. However, one rule that must be followed is that you must stand close enough to the plate so that you can cover the outside corner with the meat part of the bat. Never stand so far away that a pitch on the outside corner looks like a ball. There's no sense giving the pitcher the outside corner. It's hard enough as it is to cover the plate.

Part of your positioning depends on your stride. If you normally stride toward the plate, you can afford to stand farther away because you will still be able to cover the outside. If you have a tendency to bail out—step away—you better get up on the plate.

I stand as deep in the batter's box as I can get. Once again, you'll learn the correct spot by experimenting until you find the place that suits you.

Standing as deep as I do can hurt you sometimes. If a pitcher has a real sharp breaking curve, it could cause you trouble. Facing a pitcher like this, you might want to cheat up just a bit. I don't do it, but others do.

The reason you would move up on a good curve ball pitcher is to try to get the ball before it starts snapping. It may sound funny to you that you can actually move up that far, but you can. A good sharp curve will break most at the end of its trip, not at the beginning. From the time it leaves the pitcher's hand until it gets right out front of the plate, don't worry about it. You can't worry about what it does then because you can't hit it. It isn't there yet.

The only time you have to worry about the movement of the ball is when you can hit it with the bat. That's where it does all the sharp breaking, so moving up against the curve could help some.

Standing deep in the box does give you a few extra moments to look at the baseball. It allows you to wait just that much longer

before committing yourself. Therefore, you are harder to fool with a pitch.

BEING A SWINGER

The time now has come to swing the bat. We have found the bat we want, decided on a grip and a stance. We have our weight back and the pitcher is winding up.

Let us begin with the mind. It is bearing down on only one thing—the pitcher. Hitting is a great deal mental. You must have the two C's to hit—confidence and concentration. You can think of nothing but the ball. All the mechanics of the swing must come naturally and they will if you feel comfortable at the plate and have practiced so that the swing is second nature.

Rule Number 1 is a rule you have heard before and will hear again. Keep your eye on the ball. From the moment that baseball

THE SWING. Here is the swing as it looks to the pitcher. It all starts with the stride, as you can see. As the bat is moving into the hitting area, the hips are open and the weight is transferred to the front foot. Contact is made with the eyes right on the point of contact. Then comes the follow-through. (Photos by Fred Straub)

leaves the pitcher's hand until you have hit it, there is nothing else in the world.

This is why eyesight is so important in hitting. You must be able to distinguish between the fast ball, the curve, the slider, the knuckleball, the change-up. You must be able to decide whether it is high or low, inside or outside. You must judge the speed of the ball, its break, and make a decision to swing or not to swing.

The total time you have to make this decision is roughly four-tenths of a second. That is why total concentration is necessary. That is why it is necessary to have the mechanics down so they come naturally. That is why you must be able to see the ball.

I can see the stitches on the baseball as it comes to the plate. By the time it is halfway home, I know what kind of pitch it is. This comes from good eyesight and experience. The stitches rotate differently on each type of pitch; only by hitting time after time against all kinds of pitches can you distinguish so quickly what is coming.

You do not pick the baseball up halfway home. You pick it up as soon as it leaves the man's hand. You never take your eye off the baseball.

As a kid, this rule was drilled into me, so much so that when I take a pitch, I follow it all the way into the catcher's glove. It's something I advise. You can't take your eye off the ball too quickly if you follow it all the way to the catcher.

Now the pitch is on the way and you have decided to swing. How do you do it? You begin with the stride and, as I said, I prefer to keep the stride short.

As you begin to stride and move forward, there is one thing I must stress. The hands remain back and cocked. This is the secret to hitting. Hitting is all in the hands. Hands are the key to my theory, and to use the hands properly, they must remain uncommitted until the final second.

As you begin striding, the hips begin opening, leading the way. If the hips are locked, there is no way you can swing properly.

Let me emphasize here, though, that at no time is any of this in your mind. You can't hit a baseball moving at 90 miles an hour thinking about your feet, your head, your hands, your hips. You can only think about the ball.

THE STRIDE. Here is a closeup of the stride that should be taken by a hitter. Notice how short I stride, no more than six inches. Also, the weight transfers from the back leg to the front as you swing, the back heel actually rising off the. ground. (Photos by Fred Straub)

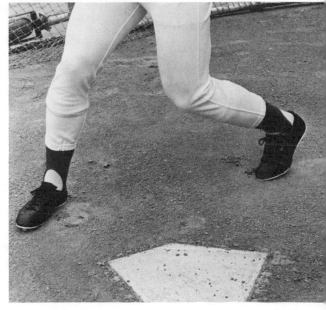

Practice. That is the answer to keeping your mind clear. Everything will come naturally once you have practiced and practiced and practiced.

How should you swing? There are many different theories here. Ted Williams, a power hitter, believes in a slight upward arc on the swing. I disagree.

I believe in a level swing, possibly even somewhat on a downward arc. The hands, which remained back, start from the top, about shoulder high. I throw my hands right out front and then go on through.

The idea is to hit the ball out front of the plate. The reason is that this is the area—about 15 inches covering the front of the plate—where the bat speed is the greatest.

As contact is made with the baseball, the arms are fully extended. The head remains on the ball. Your weight is transferred to the front foot.

Now get this. *The wrists play no part in hitting the baseball.* There is a terrible myth about the wrists being the source of your power. Henry Aaron, the greatest example, is said to be a "wrist hitter." That is impossible. Henry Aaron is merely strong and has tremendous bat speed.

The wrists, you see, remain unbroken until after contact is made with the ball. They roll only after the ball has been hit, giving you the proper follow-through.

Take the bat all the way around on the follow-through. Don't stop just as you hit the ball. That cuts down on power and will serve to louse up the rest of your swing.

That's it. Hit the ball and run as hard as you can. And, from reading this, don't become psyched out. It sounds complicated but really it isn't. Practice it again and again until you have it right and then forget about it.

(Facing page) HITTING AREA. This is the position the bat should be in as it makes contact with the ball. The arms are extended and the wrists not yet snapped. (Photo by Fred Straub)

FOLLOW-THROUGH. This is how you will look after you have completed the swing, the bat all the way around on the other side of your body. Hopefully you will be looking at a line drive. (Photo by Fred Straub)

IN SUMMARY

Here are the basics of hitting:

1. Select a comfortable bat, comfortable grip, comfortable stance and comfortable position in the batter's box.

2. Concentrate on the baseball from the time it leaves the pitcher's hand until it reaches the catcher's glove or is hit.

3. The swing starts with the stride.

4. The hips begin opening at roughly the same time.

5. The hands remain back. That is the secret to good hitting.

6. The swing takes a somewhat downward arc, the hands throwing the bat out front of the plate.

7. Hit the ball out front when the bat has the greatest speed.

8. The wrists snap just after the ball is hit and bring the bat all the way through.

chapter four

Who was the best hitter I've ever seen? I'm glad you asked that question because I have the answer.

Roberto Clemente.

It may seem a bit strange that my answer should be Clemente, a man who seemingly did everything wrong at the plate. He would lunge at the baseball. He'd hit off his front foot. He would swing at ridiculously bad pitches.

But Roberto Clemente hit the ball hard more consistently than anyone I've ever seen. He wasn't a power hitter, but he had power. What he did is just what I'd like to see every hitter do, although every hitter cannot hit like Roberto Clemente or like Pete Rose.

While Clemente was doing all those things wrong at times, he did one thing right and it is the thing I tried to get across to you in the last

hitting: an advanced study

chapter. He kept his hands back. He was fooled a lot and committed himself with his feet and his body.

But his hands were back, the trigger was cocked. He had all of his swing left. His hands enabled him to get tremendous speed out of the heavy bat he used, even when he was fooled and off balance.

Roberto Clemente had a style all his own. All the great hitters do. It is what you should do, too. You must develop your own style. Don't copy the stars. Remember, they are doing what is comfortable for them, not necessarily what will be comfortable for you.

For every great hitter, there is a different style. Steve Garvey of the Dodgers, the 1974 Most Valuable Player in the National League, hits much as I do. He stays back, hits the ball hard and sprays it all over the field.

Then you have Billy Williams, formerly of the Cubs and now with Oakland. He has the perfect swing. Small step, quick bat, light bat, swings only at strikes, and the ball jumps off his bat.

You also have Ralph Garr of the Braves, who won the 1974 National League batting title. He's a lot like Clemente in that he's a bad ball hitter. He tries to hit the ball on the ground and use his speed. Then you have guys like Rod Carew, the American League batting champion, or the Dodgers' Bill Buckner, who spray the ball around.

And, of course, you have your Willie Stargells and Willie McCoveys, straight pull hitters who want only to hit the baseball out of the park.

TO PULL OR NOT TO PULL

What is there about my style of hitting—hitting the ball hard and where it is pitched—that makes it the best way to hit, at least in my mind?

One thing and one thing only. I feel by hitting the ball with authority and not being labeled a pull hitter, the other team cannot defense you. The outfielders must play deep and pretty much straight away and that leaves wide gaps between them.

If you are a pull hitter, the defense bunches on you in one direction. You must try to hit the ball between fielders who are close together. Your chances of getting a hit—and an extra-base hit—are lessened.

The advantage of being a pull hitter, of course, is power. By that I mean home run power. If you are strong enough to reach the fence regularly, then by all means, go ahead and pull the ball and go for the homer. But don't expect to hit .300. You have to be some kind of hitter to allow the defense to overshift on you, challenge it, and come out with a strong average and a high home run total.

Hitting the ball hard is most important. If you are known as a slap hitter, you'll find the defense bunching on you as they do on a power hitter. The outfielders play shallower, leaving you less room to bloop one in. It also cuts down the gaps to the left and right of center.

I guess what I really am saying is to be aggressive at the plate. Attack the baseball. Make the defense respect you.

SHOULD I SWING ONLY AT STRIKES?

The answer to this question is yes, but the meaning of strike is a different one from the ordinary. The umpire's strike zone and the hitter's strike zone may be very different.

Earlier I called Roberto Clemente the greatest hitter I had ever seen. What do you think his lifetime batting average would have been if he'd only swung at pitches in the strike zone? Clemente finished his career with a .317 lifetime average. If he had been selective and swung only at strikes, I believe he would have hit no more than .275.

Being selective would have taken away Clemente's aggressiveness at the plate. He was what is called a "bad ball hitter." So was Yogi Berra. So is Ralph Garr.

The name, however, is misleading. The pitches these men swung at were balls, but they weren't bad balls for the hitters. These men knew their own "strike zone."

I chase "bad" pitches. They are, however, pitches I have learned I can hit. The more you hit, the more you learn which pitches you hit best. Maybe it will be that you should be like Joe Morgan of the Reds and swing only at strikes. Or maybe you are the kind of hitter who can handle the pitch up around your eyes. If you can handle it, go to it. Attack. Be aggressive.

THINKING AND HITTING

The story is an old one, but it serves its purpose well. As previously noted, Yogi Berra, back when he played for the Yankees, was a notorious bad ball hitter. During his rookie season, he went into a terrible slump and was chasing everything thrown up to the plate.

"Yogi," said Bucky Harris, then the Yankee manager, "you're not thinking up there at the plate. You have to think, think, think."

Berra promptly went to the plate, took three fast balls right down the middle and came walking back to the dugout.

"Bucky," said Yogi, "I just can't think and hit at the same time."

In a lot of ways, Yogi was right. I try to clear my mind when I'm hitting, concentrating only on the ball. But to hit well, you must think. Hitting, you see, is a case of situations. You have to know the pitcher and you have to know what he's going to throw you in a given situation.

That's why the longer a pitcher is in the league, the more success you should have with him. Pitchers, believe it or not, develop patterns. You learn the patterns, study the pitcher and how he's pitched you, and you have an advantage.

Take guys like Tom Seaver and Bob Gibson. I've hit off them for 12 years now. I have a good idea of how they're going to pitch me. That's why I have more success off them than I have off a rookie who has been in the league only two months. He doesn't have any pattern yet.

For example, against Seaver, you can bet with a man on third base and less than two out, you will not see a pitch above the knees and he will usually go with his hard stuff. With a man on second and less than two out with a weaker hitter behind you, you can be sure you won't get a good pitch to hit.

When you're hitting, you have to put all that to work for you. Before you step into the box, you think about the pitcher, what he has working for him, what he has done with you in the past, how many out, how many on.

However, once you step in, you are concentrating only on the baseball.

SHOULD I GUESS AT THE PLATE?

The best advice I can give anyone is not to guess hit. A lot of guys are successful guess hitters. I'm not saying it's right or wrong. It just isn't for me and I don't believe it is the right way to hit.

My advice to a man who wants to be a good hitter is to always look for a fast ball. You can adjust to off-speed pitches. That's just common sense. If you're up there and the man is throwing the ball 90 miles an hour and you're thinking curve, there's no way you can react.

The opposite isn't true. If you are looking for a fast ball and you are geared for it and the pitcher throws a slower curve, you can adjust and still hit the ball.

Common sense.

Most home run hitters will guess. Well, maybe you shouldn't call it guessing. They look for a certain pitch in a certain situation. You get guys like Johnny Bench and Willie Stargell, who may look for a 3-and-0 curve ball in a certain area. If they get it, look out. If they don't get it, they take the pitch.

Me, I can't do that. If I do and get the pitch I'm looking for, I think I might be right if I guess again.

Guess hitting is the reason you see a lot of good hitters take third strikes on fast balls right down the middle. They are looking for a curve and the fast ball ties them in a knot.

To put it simply, when I'm at the plate, I'm thinking fast ball, get a pitch to hit and be quick with the bat. If you are swinging good, you will be quick. Quickness means bat speed and bat speed means hitting the ball hard.

Of course, sometimes you outsmart yourself. Thinking can hurt at times. Here's an example. Joe Morgan is out of the lineup and a weaker hitter is behind me in the Cincinnati lineup. There is a man on second and less than two out.

"There's no way they're going to give me a pitch to hit. They're going to pitch around me," I tell myself.

Next thing I know, I've taken two fast balls right down the middle. I've outsmarted myself. Instead of going to the plate with the idea of hitting, I went up expecting not to be hitting. I put myself in a hole.

HITTING WITH TWO STRIKES

The first thing to remember here is that a strikeout is not the end of the world. Therefore, you don't want to become too defensive at the plate. You are still looking to get a base hit, not just to keep from striking out.

What you do is cut down just a hair on your swing. You keep it short and compact, yet you remain with the idea of hitting the ball hard. Many times I've hit 395-foot fly balls with two strikes on me that would have been home runs if I had had one strike on me.

The reason is that I cut down on the swing. Yet, I wasn't so defensive that I was just slapping at the ball. There are many hitters who cut down on their swing so much that they are totally defensive hitters. They are the guys who usually are in the top five of not striking out—Tommy Helms, Glenn Beckert, Felix Millan, Matty Alou. They don't strike out, but they don't hit with power, either. They are the kind of guys who don't get a man in from third base with a deep fly ball.

HITTING 'EM WHERE THEY AIN'T

The key to a high batting average is to make the defense play you wrong. The best way to do this is to make sure there is no right way to play you. If you sometimes hit the ball to right field, sometimes to left, sometimes to center, sometimes bunt, sometimes hit and run, and sometimes hit the home run, you present the defense with a problem.

But this is easier said than done. You must know how to hit the ball where you want to hit it.

The secret is all in the hands. Some people profess that you should step the way you are going to hit the ball. I don't believe in this. To begin with, you have to make up your mind before the pitch that you are going to go to the opposite field with the ball or that you are going to pull the ball. The baseball comes too quickly to the plate to see where the pitch is, step in the direction you want, and hit the ball that way.

Worse yet, I don't believe there are enough pitchers today who can be so consistent that I can think along with them. I can't make up my mind before I go to the plate to hit the ball to opposite field because I just may not get a pitch to hit that way, even though the pitcher is trying to keep the ball outside. He may not have good enough control. Certainly, no pitcher can stand 60 feet, 6 inches from home plate and continually throw the ball where he wants to and have something on it.

No, the correct way to hit the ball to the opposite field or to pull the ball or hit it through the middle is to use the hands. Nothing else in the swing changes.

If you are going to the opposite field, the hands are out in front of the bat so that the bat meets the ball at a bit of an angle. You still are swinging hard, but you are steering the ball.

I actually believe that by using this method, I can hit an inside pitch to the opposite field almost as well as I can an outside pitch.

Of course, this doesn't hold true when you are trying to pull the ball. It is hard to pull an outside pitch because you need such a strong top hand. Only guys like Aaron are capable of pulling the outside pitch effectively.

When pulling the ball, you use your hands. They are quick, throwing the bat out front. The fact of the matter is that sometimes it's hard to pull an inside pitch and keep the ball from going foul. There are some hitters in the league to whom the Reds try to throw one or two fast balls deep inside, knowing the best they can do is pull it foul.

Going through the middle—which I do most frequently—once again comes from those hands. The hands get the bat out front of the plate, meeting the baseball squarely.

Remember one thing about hitting. Patience pays off. One of my biggest problems comes when I feel I have to pull the ball, a runner on second and none out, trying to get him to third so he can score on a fly ball.

When I'm up in this situation, I often get all messed up, even after 12 years, because I won't wait for the good pitch to pull. If you're patient, the pitcher will come to you. It goes back to the idea that the pitcher can't consistently keep the ball away, throwing hard from 60 feet, 6 inches. If you're patient, he will make a mistake.

Patience often is the key to hitting. Henry Aaron says that every time he comes to the plate, he gets one pitch he can hit out of the ball park.

A BASE HIT. Here *(pages 42 through 44)* is a sequence of my swing on a base hit against the Montreal Expos. Observe that as I stride and begin to open my hips, the bat remains back, fully cocked. As contact is made, the bat is just about level with the ground, the wrists not yet broken and the eyes on the ball. Last comes the follow-through and the run to first. (Photos by Fred Straub)

Believe it or not, he's just about right. Oh, every once in a while, you'll run into a Nolan Ryan who is having one of those nights when his ball is moving all over the place. You'll get a strike to hit, but that doesn't mean it's a pitch to hit hard.

However, even with your good pitchers like Tom Seaver, Andy Messersmith, and Don Sutton, you will get one good pitch to hit every time up. It's your fault if you foul it off.

TAKING A STRIKE

Patience, however, doesn't mean that you should get in the habit of

taking a strike. Some hitters do it. Willie McCovey almost always takes the first pitch and Ted Williams did the same thing.

I believe it's wrong. If you were supposed to take a strike, they would have made it two strikes and you're out, not three.

In baseball, you should never give something to anyone. If they give it to you, take it. Baseball is a game of give and take and whoever takes the most is going to win.

However, I do believe in being selective at the plate. Until you have two strikes, when you must protect the plate, wait for the pitch you can hit. If it comes on the first pitch, go get it. If it comes on the third, go get it.

Remember. Be patient. You will get your pitch.

STRICTLY PERSONAL

For a moment here, we are going to get selfish. As I said, baseball is a very individual team game. My goals, for example, each year, are to hit .300, get 200 hits, and score 100 runs. Why should I set up those goals? Because each of them helps the team. I am a leadoff hitter. My job is to get on base and score runs.

Thinking about these goals, then, I consider the two most important at bats to be your first and your last in a game.

You've heard the old cliché, "You better get this guy early because the more he pitches, the better he gets." Well, I believe in it.

Good pitchers often don't get ready down in the bullpen. They need that adrenalin to get flowing in the first couple of innings to get it together.

Therefore, the first time you face a pitcher, he may not have his stuff together and it is the time to hit him. That, of course, helps the team and your batting average.

Now for the last at bat against the same pitcher. This becomes, in most instances, strictly personal. Usually, if the starter is still in there in the ninth inning, he has a commanding lead. In a 4-3 or 5-4 game, you usually are facing relief pitchers in the late innings.

This at bat, with your team trailing badly, becomes very important to the batting average, especially for a leadoff hitter who often gets one extra at bat a game.

Let me give you an illustration. A couple of years back, the Reds were trailing Atlanta and Phil Niekro, 7-2, in the ninth inning. I was 4-for-4 off Niekro, none of it helping us get a victory. Now I got that one extra at bat, that one extra chance to improve my average.

Niekro is a knuckleball pitcher. His first two pitches were knucklers and each missed the plate. I stepped out and thought to myself: "Now what's he going to throw me, winning by five runs and with a 2-0 count?"

I knew it had to be a fast ball. I hit a home run on the fast ball and it gave me a 5-for-5 day. You can bet if you face a pitcher who has a big lead that he isn't going to walk you if he can help it. He'll give you a pitch to hit and that's why you really bear down on that last at bat, especially in that situation.

THE PITCHER

I can remember the first game I ever played in the big leagues. Jocko

Conlan was the umpire, and after the game, he came over to me.

"Son," he said, "being a leadoff hitter, the best pitch you're gonna get is the one-ball, no-strike pitch leading off the game."

I thought he was crazy at the time. Everyone knows that the 2-and-0 or 3-and-1 pitch is the best to hit. But I learned differently. I have found that he is exactly right, although I can't tell you why.

For some unknown reason, 99 out of 100 times, when I'm leading off a game and take the first pitch for a ball, the next pitch is a fast ball. Why do pitchers do this? So they don't have to throw me a fast ball on the 2-and-0 pitch. They don't want to throw me a 2-0 fast ball, but they'll throw it at 1-0.

Don't, however, get the idea that pitchers are dumb. Oh, sometimes they seem that way. Take the times you see a pitcher throw a fast ball inside for a strike. Then he throws a second fast ball inside for strike two. Now he throws a third fast ball inside and the hitter is waiting for it and gets a hit.

Makes the pitcher look dumb, doesn't it? But what normally is happening here is that the pitcher merely lost a guessing game. "I've thrown him two inside fast balls, he's got to think I'm going to throw him a curve ball away," thinks the pitcher. This time he turns out wrong.

The pitcher's main problem is that he can't forever throw the ball where he wants to. If he could, he would almost always look very, very smart indeed.

The battle between the pitcher and batter is the most intriguing in all of sports. It is a physical battle, but it is also a psychological battle.

Take me. Psychologically, I prefer to hit against a pitcher who uses the no-windup delivery—just holds his hands in front of him, rocks into the motion and throws.

I just don't think a pitcher who does this can get that good kick and follow-through that a guy does who takes a full windup and gets all his momentum going. To me, a pitcher who doesn't wind up looks lazy.

Since hitting is a great deal mental and a great deal confidence, I have a large edge against a pitcher like this.

The same thing goes for a pitcher who throws straight over the top, throws hard, and has a good curve ball. I believe in myself against this type of pitcher. All it amounts to is adjustment. His curve ball will break down, not away, so merely adjust to it. A pitcher like this I find to be easier to hit than a guy who throws four or five different pitches and comes at you from different angles.

FEAR STRIKES OUT

I have no fear when I'm hitting. However, a lot of players do, even in the big leagues. They are so sacred you can knock the bat right out of their hands.

Avoiding fear goes back to one thing, believing in yourself. Confidence. You have to have the confidence that you can hit. If you have that, you don't care how hard the man throws.

Believe me, it's no fun to be hit with a baseball. But about the only place you can suffer a serious injury is if you are hit in the head and that is the hardest place to hit anyone. The only guys I've seen who have taken the ball in the head have lost sight of the pitch on its way to the plate. They didn't see it.

Sometimes, with a pitcher who is getting me out consistently, I'll start yelling at him. "You got nothing. Get that junk over." Stuff like that. I'm trying to get him mad, trying to get him to hit me.

If he does, I save an at bat and get first base. That, after all, is what it's all about.

BATTING PRACTICE

For me, the most fun part of any day during the season is batting practice. It is also one of the most important times of the day.

I am a great believer that the way you practice is the way you'll play. When I hit well in batting practice, I normally hit well in the game. The reason is that to hit well, you have to swing well. If my swing is grooved in batting practice, I believe it will be grooved during the game.

Batting practice is not a time just to see how far you can hit the

47

baseball. Work on things. I do. And it doesn't have to be an unenjoyable kind of work.

In the big leagues, we turn batting practice into a game. The prizes normally are cokes in the clubhouse. Maybe one go-round Joe Morgan and I will see how many base hits we can get to the opposite field. In another, we may see how many hits it takes to score a run.

I'll work hard on other things, such as hitting the ball to the right side with a man on second and none out, then pretending he's on third and trying to score him with a fly ball.

Usually we'll end batting practice on our final two swings by playing "long ball," seeing which one of us can hit the ball the farthest.

There is competition involved in all of this, plus the idea of working on certain skills that you will be called on to use during the game.

The one thing you don't want is a batting practice pitcher who just lollipops the baseball to the plate. You want a guy who gives you pitches to hit, but has something on the ball.

I've been accused at times of taking too much batting practice. If I have something that I want to work on, say hitting the curve or the slider, I'll come out to the ball park early and take extra batting practice for an hour. I almost always hit well during the game on a night when I take extra batting practice.

One word of caution here. If you get tired, you should quit. It doesn't do you one bit of good to be swinging the bat when your arms are weary or when your concentration has left you.

PLAYING PEPPER

Pepper is one of the finest games ever devised in baseball. It consists of a man hitting the ball to one player or a group of players. The batter stands maybe 35 feet away from the men, who catch each hit and pitch it back quickly.

This is especially good for a hitter's eyes and also his hands. It can help you be a good bunter because you learn how to put the bat on the baseball and shorten up on your swing.

The game is also good for the men who are "fielding" and it is great for pitchers. If you hit the ball firmly back at the other players, it has got to help their reflexes and their ability to pick the ball up off the bat and field their position.

chapter five

In 1969 I was the defending National League batting champion, having won my first title the season before in a tight race with Matty Alou of the Pirates. This time, the race was just as tight, me and Roberto Clemente.

It went to the final day of the season. The Reds had been eliminated from the Western Division race and were losing this game. As I went to the plate for my final at bat, I was hitless. I knew that if I went 0-for-4 and Clemente went 4-for-4, he would win the batting title.

As I kneeled in the on-deck circle, a fan in the stands with a radio leaned over and told me that Clemente was 3-for-3 in Pittsburgh with the game still going on.

I needed a hit. A man was at second and two were out. Normally,

the lost art of bunting

in this situation, I'd be swinging away, trying to drive in a run. But we could do no better than finish third and we were losing the final game of the season.

I decided right then that I was going to bunt. I went up, laid down a perfect bunt toward third base, beat it out without so much as a throw, and cinched the batting title.

I use this example to let you know just how important a bunt can be. For me, it meant a batting title, and over a season, I can't tell you how many games it decides. In fact, I consider the two most important plays in baseball to be the bunt and the double play. With all the games that are decided nowadays by one run, the bunt becomes a crucial play.

Usually, it is the pitcher who is called on to sacrifice bunt. It is his chance—normally being a weak offensive player—to help himself. This is especially true when you have a hitter like me or Lou Brock coming up next, guys who get 200 hits a year.

It never ceases to amaze me how many guys can't bunt, though, especially pitchers. To me, it is one of the easiest things in the game to do.

There are two basic types of bunts: the sacrifice and the bunt for a hit. First we will discuss the sacrifice.

THE SACRIFICE BUNT

The most important thing to remember here is that a sacrifice bunt is just what the name implies. You are sacrificing yourself, giving yourself up to move a runner up a base. Your only concern is with moving the runner along, not beating out the bunt.

There are two ways to sacrifice. The way the Reds teach is to turn only the upper half of the body toward the pitcher while keeping the feet planted. The other way is to rotate the hips and move the feet so they are parallel to the plate. How should you do it? Whichever way you can get the ball down best. We are interested in results. The reason most teams now are teaching the method of merely turning the upper half of the body is that it can be done a split second later, thereby not giving away the sacrifice quite so quickly. However, most sacrifice situations are readily obvious to the defense and they won't often be fooled.

Whichever way you decide to turn, you should wind up looking straight ahead at the pitcher with both eyes. The bat is held level with the ground—most important—and you hold it chest high—even more important.

(Facing page) SACRIFICING. Here are two views of the sacrifice bunt. Note the way the bat is held high in the strike zone, parallel to the ground. The knees are flexed and the bat gripped softly in the hands. The bat is pinched right at the trademark by the top hand, which will give as the ball is bunted to deaden the bunt. (Photos by Fred Straub)

With the bat at the top of the strike zone, any pitch that is higher than the bat is a ball and you will not try to bunt at it. It is always easier to go down after a pitch than it is to come up after one, because you bend your knees.

If you begin with the bat down by the knees and get a letter-high fast ball to bunt, the best you will do is pop it foul. You will be unable to bunt the pitch on the ground.

Your bottom hand remains in place as you grip the bat. The top hand slides down to the bat's trademark. Do not wrap your fingers around the bat. Instead, pinch it between your thumb and index finger. This helps deaden the ball as it hits the bat and it prevents you from having your fingers smashed—a most unpleasant thing.

The bat is held firmly, but not with a death grip. You don't want the ball rattling the bat in your hand, but you also don't want it to be a ground ball to shortstop. Practice will let you know when you are holding the bat with the right firmness.

One thing to avoid is going out after the ball. That is incorrect. You let the ball come to the bat. The movement is from the top down. Not out toward the pitch. Stabbing at the ball with the bat makes it almost impossible to deaden the ball or guide it.

You steer the bunt with your bottom hand. If you want to bunt toward first and are a right-handed hitter, you push the bottom hand forward so the bat meets the ball at an angle. Pull back with the bottom hand when you want to go toward third base, again giving angle to the bat. All the while, though, the bat remains level with the ground.

One rule that must be followed—and one of the hardest rules to follow—is that you must get a strike to bunt. If the pitch is out of the strike zone, pull off.

Believe me, bunting just isn't as hard as people make it look. One thing you will find is that if you turn around and face the pitcher, the ball comes to the plate looking as if it has nothing on it. It's just like when you're taking a 3-and-0. The ball then always looks like a little fast ball down the middle.

Most of the time in a sacrifice situation, you will be given a fast ball to bunt. The toughest pitch to bunt is a fast ball that is high, since this pitch usually is popped up.

But you should never pop up a bunt. Never. Not if you start with the bat at the letters and bunt at nothing but strikes.

Things change just a little on the suicide squeeze play. You must wait until the final second before committing yourself, unless you want the pitcher throwing that fast ball right between your eyes. And, no matter where the pitch is, you bunt it. You don't get fancy, either. Just get the ball on the ground in fair territory and it's a run for your side.

THE BUNT FOR A HIT

There are two types of bunts for a hit, the drag or the push bunt. On the drag bunt, you do just what the name implies: you try to drag the ball past the pitcher's mound and make the second baseman field the ball if you are a left-handed hitter. On the push bunt, a left-handed hitter bunts the ball toward third base.

Normally you have made up your mind before you step into the box whether you are going to bunt for a hit or not and which bunt you will use.

The defense usually dictates this.

As a left-handed hitter, you might drop one toward third if you find the third baseman playing too deep to throw you out. Sometimes, I'll try to bunt toward third even if the man is in—because of the element of surprise. Playing in, he doesn't really expect you to bunt and might be taken by surprise. But, if you do it in this situation, you must get a good pitch to bunt because you have to make a nearly perfect bunt.

The one thing I haven't done much has been drag the ball past the pitcher; and it is something I plan to do more of. On AstroTurf, the second basemen are playing so deep that they are taking hits away from me. A couple of drag bunts for hits might make the second basemen move in a step or two and cut down on their range.

On both types of bunts, you are moving toward first base before you actually have bunted the ball. As soon as you see where the pitch is, you are moving. That means just about as soon as the pitch leaves the pitcher's hand, you begin for first base.

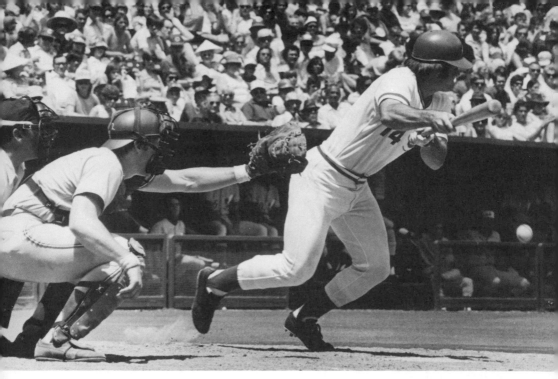

BUNTING FOR A HIT. When bunting for a hit, the element of surprise is important. Notice that the catcher was totally caught here, not at all moving forward even after the ball has already been bunted. I am off and running as soon as the ball is bunted. Also notice that I have watched the ball all the way to the bat. The bat is out of my hands before I have taken two steps. Now it is full speed to first base. (Photos by Fred Straub)

If the pitch is inside, you can leave a little quicker. If it is outside, you have to wait just a fraction of a second more to make sure you can reach the ball.

If the pitch is a curve ball, it is a little easier to bunt than the fast ball, but you have to wait a little longer. That's the big problem bunting this way, the waiting. You are so eager to get a flying start that sometimes you outrun the ball to the plate. You must show patience.

On the push bunt toward third, you try to deaden the ball so that all the third baseman can do is make a running, bare-handed play. On the drag, you want to hit the ball firmly enough to make sure the pitcher cannot get to it. The second baseman must field the ball for the bunt to be a success.

PRACTICE DOES MAKE PERFECT

Bunting, as I said, is not a difficult thing to do. But it does take practice. I believe the reason so many big leaguers don't bunt well is that they don't practice enough.

Pitchers probably ought to bunt 25 balls a day—this can be done off a pitching machine—to make sure that they can get a man over whenever called on. They should practice bunting toward third, as they will with men at first and second, and bunting toward first, as they will with a man on first.

They can drop a towel on the field where they want to try and stop the ball and shoot for that. But practice is vital. It is something the Dodgers of 1974 did very well and they won the Western Division championship from us by four games. At least that many games were decided because we just couldn't get a man over when we wanted to.

Any player with extreme speed would do well to practice bunting for a base hit. Bobby Tolan did this in 1970, when he led the league in stolen bases, and wound up getting nearly 20 bunt singles. That may have added as many as 30 points to his batting average and gave him that many more chances to steal a base and score a run.

The Reds right now have a young player named Ken Griffey who can really fly. He is being asked to spend a half hour a day practicing bunting. If he can learn to bunt, he has a chance to be a .300 hitter.

chapter six

Seems like every time I get myself involved in something controversial, it happens because I was running the bases aggressively. It goes back to my belief in the way the game should be played . . . all the way, full speed.

In 1970, depending on whether you were an American League or a National League fan, I became a villain or a hero when I scored the winning run in the All-Star game by slamming into the Cleveland catcher, Ray Fosse, in the 10th inning.

In 1973, I became a big bully for sliding hard into Bud Harrelson of the New York Mets, trying to break up a double play. We wound up in a tremendous fight and the effects of that conflict have yet to wear off.

Each of those plays carried lessons I would like to get across to

run for the money

you about base running. The first lesson is always to go all out. The second lesson is always to be thinking. The third lesson is to go, go, go when it will take a perfect play to get you out.

In both plays, I went all out. In the play with Fosse, it paid off. I was safe and the game was won. In the Harrelson play, I was out and I didn't break up the double play. But no one can criticize me for not trying.

In both plays I was thinking. Consider for a moment the play in the 1970 All-Star game. I was at second when Jim Hickman of the Chicago Cubs singled. First, I knew that two were out and if I stopped at third, we needed yet another hit to drive me in. Second, I knew that the game was on the line. I knew what kind of arm the outfielder had and I knew it would take a perfect play to get me.

So, I took the chance. Normally, on a two-out single, I can score from second base without much trouble. But we were on AstroTurf, the ball was a one-hopper, and it was fielded perfectly.

In fact, it was a perfect play on both sides. The outfielder had a nice arm and made a perfect throw. I just happened to beat it by a fraction of a second, allowing me to hit Fosse just before the ball arrived.

Normally, on a play as close as that one, I would slide. I actually started to do a head-first slide into the plate until I saw Fosse had the plate blocked. All I could have done was challenge two hard plastic shin guards with my head, so I went in standing up and the collision was one heard all around the world.

In the Harrelson episode, once again I was thinking. I was on first and we were hopelessly out of the third game of the playoffs. Joe Morgan hit a ground ball to the first baseman behind me. I couldn't see if he had stepped on first base and then thrown to second—meaning I had to be tagged—or if he had thrown to second without touching the base—meaning Harrelson had to return the ball to first for a double play.

I decided that I had to go in hard, trying to knock the ball loose if I had to be tagged, and I had to use a pop-up slide in an effort to keep Harrelson from throwing to first.

I was too late. I got there after the throw was off and when I popped up, my elbow accidentally caught Harrelson in the face. Hence, the fight.

GETTING AWAY FROM THE PLATE

Running the bases begins as soon as you hit the ball. The first thing you have to remember is that there is nothing you can do about the baseball once you hit it. Therefore, don't look at it.

Looking at the ball costs you speed, and speed is vital, especially on an infield grounder. If it goes through, the first base coach will let you know in plenty of time to make a turn.

On an infield grounder, only one thought should be on your mind—getting to first base as fast as you can. Never curse your bad luck of hitting a routine grounder. Always go full speed and hope for a bobble by the infielder that allows you to reach base. By going all out, you might even *cause* the bobble, making the man rush more than he wants to in fielding the ball.

When you reach the base, your object is to hit the front half of it with either foot. You hit the front half of the bag because that is closer to you; therefore, it takes you that much less time to get there and gives you that much more of an edge.

Remember, the more hits you get that you shouldn't get, the higher your average will be. Hustle always. Make things happen. Usually when you make things happen, they happen in your favor.

THE BASE HIT

There is no such thing as a single. At least that's what should be in your mind when you hit what seems to be a single. You just don't think single. Think double. Always be thinking of making an extra base on a ball you hit safely. You see so many guys line one to left, jog to first, make a little turn, and then watch the outfielder misplay the ball. All they can do is return to first.

Rounding first base is tricky and very important if you are going to try for a double. You take a little dip out of the base line just before reaching the base. The closer to the base you can do it, the better.

Ideally, you hit the base with your left—or inside—foot and turn as tightly as possible so you are heading almost directly toward second base. If, for some reason, you are off stride and must hit the base with your right foot, go ahead and do it. Don't change stride just to touch the base with the inside foot. You will lose more time than you save.

I pick the ball up with my eyes as I make the turn. And, I am thinking about going to second base. I don't stop my momentum until I make my turn and see that the outfielder has caught the ball.

What are you looking for when you are thinking of stretching the hit? The first thing, of course, is the outfielder missing the ball. If he does that, you're gone.

Even if he catches the ball, you might keep right on going for a second if you've noticed that man has been slow fielding the ball. If he waited back, thinking it is only a single, you might be able to make it.

If the ball is hit in the alley, make the outfielder throw the ball. Dare him. And, if you believe the only way he can get you out is with a perfect throw, take the chance and go. I know how hard it is to make the perfect throw.

Remember, though, that the situation will dictate your moves. Later we'll go into the situations where it is unwise to gamble.

There are other factors that you may want to take advantage of. Perhaps you know the outfielder has hurt his arm and can't throw well. You might then want to run on him.

Or maybe he's a hot-headed sort of guy who struck out the inning before. If he's mad, he might not even be paying any attention to what he's doing out there in the field and you can take advantage of this.

Whatever the case, get the reputation of being the kind of player who will stretch a single into a double or a double into a triple. If you do that, you make the guys in the field hurry, and when they hurry, they can make a mistake.

TAKING A LEAD

The question here is a simple one. How far off the base can I get? My answer is that an appropriate lead puts you off the base far enough that you have to take one step and dive to get back. That's a base stealer's lead.

However, everyone isn't capable of taking this kind of lead. Everyone's reactions are different. When stealing or getting back on a throw over to first from the pitcher, you are reacting to his moves. If you don't have good reactions, you must take less of a lead. The trick is to get far enough off the base so that you feel relaxed.

You should never get off so far that your first reaction is back toward the base. That defeats the purpose. You get off far enough so you know you can get back safely, yet don't have to be leaning back toward the base to do it.

62

THE PROPER LEAD. Here, in a game against Montreal, I have my lead off first base. Note the way I am concentrating on the pitcher and ready to break in either direction. This lead is not a base stealer's lead. A base stealer would be off at least two more feet. (Photo by Fred Straub)

The lead from second base is totally different from the lead from first. I get off the base about 12 feet or so. Normally, you are watching the second baseman and the third base coach is watching the shortstop for you. If he hollers, "Get back," you do it in a hurry because you know the shortstop is cutting in behind you.

With Johnny Bench batting, the shortstop plays way over in the hole because Bench is a right-handed pull hitter. Therefore, I don't have to worry about him. I do, however, have to cut my lead down because the second baseman is playing over near the base.

63

It works the opposite way with Joe Morgan hitting. Then the second baseman plays toward first and I don't have to worry about him, but the shortstop is in near the base and he is my concern.

The one thing I don't like to be doing when leading off second base is jockeying back and forth and jumping around. You get a good, solid lead and then go with the pitch. Don't bounce around out there on the base paths.

When leading, your weight is evenly balanced on both feet, the knees bent. You remain on the balls of your feet, relaxed, yet ready to react.

The first step, whether it be back to the base on a pick-off or toward the next base, is taken with the back foot. If returning to first, you cross over with your right foot. If going toward second, you cross over with your left. Always use the crossover step. If you begin by stepping with the foot nearest the place you are going, you can take only half a step and have no drive. I would estimate it costs you a full stride and that is usually the difference between being safe and being out.

LEGAL ROBBERY

You have your lead off first base. What, however, are you thinking about? Your main concern at this point is the pitcher. The thing to do is study the pitcher.

If you are a smart base runner, you have studied the pitcher from the dugout. With a new pitcher, a lot of good base runners (like Lou Brock or Joe Morgan) will make the man throw to first so they can see his move.

If he has a tricky move—like Roger Craig or Warren Spahn used to have—you really bear down. Guys like that can pick you off in a hurry if you aren't concentrating.

Always you are trying to find some giveaway that gives you an advantage. Some pitchers never throw to first base. Some pitchers will give you a little double jerk of the head when going home. Some pitchers will never throw to the plate without looking at first, but won't throw to first once they look over there.

If you spot anything like this, you are in charge. Stealing becomes almost easy because you can get a tremendous jump.

There are three things you want when stealing. You want as long a lead as you can get, as good a jump as you can get, and as bad a throw from the catcher as you can get.

Even a slow runner can steal bases, if he can get the big lead and the big jump. You steal off the pitcher and not the catcher.

With a right-hander, it is often best to watch his left shoulder. He can't come to first base without moving that shoulder toward the base and he can't go to the plate after moving the shoulder toward the base. That would be a balk.

A pitcher can balk in many ways. The balk is in the rule book to protect the runner. It requires that the pitcher make no deceptive move. He cannot bluff you to the base in any way and then go home.

I actually prefer to have a left-hander on the mound over a right-hander. A right-hander has his back to you while a left-hander is facing you. You see the whole picture on a left-hander.

Once you break on the steal, never look back. It doesn't matter where the pitch is. You just go full speed and slide in hard. You watch the man covering the base because he will let you know whether the throw is on the money or off to one side. That will dictate which way you slide.

SLIDING

If ever there was an important rule in baseball, it is this one: When in doubt, slide. It is always better to slide on a close play. You should never be tagged out without sliding into a base; and sliding, of course, keeps you from over-running the bag.

Ever since I played knothole ball, I have done my sliding head first. It just came naturally to me and I consider it the best way to slide. To begin with, I believe by diving head first for the bag, you actually pick up momentum and get there faster.

Another thing is that you can see the ball when it gets away from the fielder, giving you the opportunity to bounce up quickly and move up an extra base. If you rely on the coach to tell you the ball

THE "BELLY-WHOPPER." Here I come scoring a run against San Francisco with a head-first slide, the way I believe it is best to slide. Note that I am ready to land on my forearms and elbows, not on my belly. (Photo by Bob Free)

has gotten loose, you lose valuable time and may not be able to make it.

I also believe it is a safe way to slide. You might get spiked on the fingers or the hand, but that isn't too serious an injury. If you slide feet first, you can get spiked on the ankle and it could take a while to shake an injury like that, because the ankle supports the weight of your body.

Of course, you won't be breaking any legs sliding head first either. Most injuries while sliding come from indecision. The runner isn't sure and only half-slides, catching his spikes and breaking the ankle. That's why I say if there's any doubt, slide.

I've never been hurt sliding head first. Of course, I don't slide head first when breaking up a double play or coming into home plate. If you do it coming into the plate, you're likely to wind up smashing your face into the catcher's shin guards. Your legs are more durable for such punishment than your nose and chin.

To call the head-first slide a belly-whopper, as so many people do, is wrong. You actually break your dive by landing on your forearms and knees.

There are other slides, all valuable to know. The first is the pop-up slide. You go in with your right leg extended and the left leg bent under it. Your momentum, as you hit the base, forces you right back up again.

This slide is good because you're not lying there on your back looking at the sky. You can see the ball get loose and are ready to take off again. It's the best kind of slide to use when stealing.

There is also the hook slide. You throw your weight to either side—the opposite side of where the throw is—hit the corner of the base with your foot, and hook around the bag. This way, you give the fielder very little to tag.

You can also slide past the base and reach back with your hand. I don't like this kind of slide because you waste time, not touching the base until your body already is past it, and because the umpires have a tendency to call you out anyway, thinking that you should have been out.

DANCING IS A CONTACT SPORT

Baseball is not a contact sport. Dancing is. Baseball, instead, is a collision sport. And there are two plays when you can expect a collision. One is breaking up a double play, the other is when you and the ball arrive at home plate at the same time.

In trying to break up a double play, it has gotten to the point nowadays where very few players are sliding into the base. What you are trying to do is hit the man making the throw, either keeping him from throwing or forcing him to throw wildly.

I believe that you go in on this play knees first. Never go in with your spikes high. You're trying to break up a double play, not trying to hurt anyone. I don't even believe in a rolling block at second. That can cause injury.

Most of the time, you aim your slide for the spot you think the player will be in. Of course, you don't go far enough away from the bag to have interference called on you. You slide where you think you can make contact with the man.

It's easier to break up the double play when the second baseman is the pivot man. The shortstop is coming right at you. He can see you and jump over you or out of the way before you get a piece of him.

The second baseman, though, doesn't see you. Often he's planted on the base, so when you hit him, he can't get off the throw.

Most of your collisions at the plate come when trying to score from second base on a single. With less than two out, you try to get the biggest lead you can, because often you will hold up to make sure the ball is a hit. If there are two out, of course, you are running on the crack of the bat.

When the coach waves you around third, you begin looking for the on-deck hitter. He is supposed to be at the plate, signaling to you whether or not you should slide.

Once you catch his signal, you look for the catcher. From his reaction, you can see which way you are going to slide.

Most times coming into the plate, you slide because it's the proper thing to do. When in doubt, slide, remember. But if I see I'm not going to make it with a slide because the catcher is blocking the plate, I try to bowl him over. I don't like to do that, but if the catcher is going to mess with the bull, he's going to get the horns.

This is what happened on the play with Fosse. We both were injured and that's why you try to avoid this when possible. But, if it's impossible, let him know that he was in a collision.

GOING FROM FIRST TO THIRD

I'm not known as a good base stealer, but I am known as a good base runner. There's a big difference. I'm a good base runner because I'm aggressive. I stretch singles into doubles and I go from first to third on base hits, sometimes on hits that would move other players only to second base.

Going from first to third doesn't necessarily depend on the jump you get when the ball is hit. More important is going from first to second quickly, making a tight turn and then really turning it on for third.

You have to make up your mind that you're going to third as soon as the ball is hit unless the hit is to left field and the play is in front of you. Before the ball is hit, you know exactly where the outfielders are playing and what kind of arms they have. And, of course, you know the situation.

As a rule of thumb, never get thrown out at third base as the first or third out of an inning. That isn't the time to gamble. Another rule: Don't get thrown out at second leading off the inning.

With two out and a weak hitter coming up, gamble. Especially if you are trying to score a run.

If you trail in a game by two runs or more, never gamble. You don't want to take your team out of a possible big inning by being thrown out on the bases. You want to make the pitcher earn all the outs he is to get.

BEING SMART

One of the toughest plays in baseball is to keep from being doubled off base on a line drive. Naturally, when a ball is hit sharply, the first reaction is to run. It is a reaction that must be suppressed.

One way to keep this from happening to you is to make sure you know where every player is playing. That will help. Another way is to tell yourself to make sure the ball gets through on a line drive every time you reach base.

THE SLIDE. I don't always slide head first, as evidenced by this play at the plate. Notice that Joe Morgan, the next hitter, has signaled me to stand up. But, as I have stated, when in doubt it's best to slide, and from watching the catcher I thought there might be a play on me. Here I am just beginning to bench my right leg under, and you can see from the position of the right foot that there is no way I'm going to catch my spikes in the dirt. (Photo by Fred Straub)

As I said, going from first to third doesn't depend as much on the jump you get as on how hard you run. Make sure. Don't get doubled off on a line drive if it can be avoided.

One final point on running the bases. You must train yourself when on third base to go back to the bag and tag up on a fly ball— every fly ball.

As soon as the ball is hit in the air, you retreat to the base and take a position as if you are going to get a stand-up start in a race. As soon as the ball is caught, you go. Don't cheat or be too anxious. Make sure the ball hits the outfielder's glove, then go.

I like to watch the play, rather than to depend on the coach. Once again, you have to know the situation. How does the fielder throw? What is the score? Who is the next hitter? You make up your own mind whether you can make it or not. Always, however, make the man throw the ball. Remember, when you make things happen, they usually happen in your favor. Even when you bluff, watch the ball. If it's mishandled, you might be able to score.

Base running will decide a lot of games over an entire season. The more things you make happen, the more runs you will score. Stretch a leadoff single into a double, and all of a sudden, you can score without a hit. A ground ball to the right side and a sacrifice fly can produce a run.

Beat out an infield hit in a tie game and the world will love you. Don't hustle on a ground ball and you'll be booed by your own sister.

chapter seven

In 1971 Bob Howsam, who runs the Cincinnati Reds, made a trade with the San Diego Padres. He sent a little-used reserve outfielder named Angel Bravo to the Padres for Al Ferrara, a powerful pinch-hitter type who had a reputation as something less than an adept fielder.

We got to Philadelphia one day and for some reason, Ferrara found himself in left field. Two fly balls were hit his way. On each, he made spectacular diving catches. Trouble was, each was a routine fly ball. He circled them, misjudged them, and then had to dive for them.

After the game, the reporters gathered around The Bull, as we called Ferrara, and asked him about his two catches. Ferrara looked up from his locker and said:

playing the outfield

"What'd ya expect for Angel Bravo? Willie Mays?"

Indeed. Everyone can't be a Willie Mays or a Roberto Clemente. But anyone with some speed and athletic ability can play defensive baseball. We will start with playing the outfield.

I started my career as an infielder. I was, in fact, National League Rookie of the Year as a second baseman and made the All-Star team. I now play third base.

I have played all of the outfield positions, last settling in left field.

THE STANCE

Playing the outfield begins with the stance. I suggest that you plant

AT THE READY. In the outfield you will crouch with your hands on your knees, concentrating on the hitter. Note that you are on the balls of your feet, ready to make a move. This is the proper stance in the outfield. (Photo by Fred Straub)

your feet about shoulder-width apart and square toward home plate. Not that everyone does it this way. Willie Stargell, for example, stands with his back toward the left-field line. I don't like that because I don't believe you can go to the line as quickly as you can when you are facing the plate.

Your weight should be forward, on the balls of the feet. You are ready to move in any direction. The one thing you want to avoid—and leaning forward some with the knees bent and the weight on the balls of the feet will help—is taking a step back on every ball that is hit.

Your hands can either be on your knees or held in front of your body. It depends on which way is most comfortable for you. I prefer my hands on my knees.

The most important thing about the stance is that it puts you in a position to move—and movement is the key to outfield play. You have to get to the ball, and the time you save with your start could be the difference between making a play or not making one.

GOING AFTER THE BALL

The first thing you should be aware of when talking about defensive play is that you must stay off your heels. Always be on the balls of your feet.

This helps you in many ways. When running after a fly ball on the heels, you will take jarring steps and the ball will seem to "bounce" as it floats through the air. It is harder to judge.

Being on the balls of the feet also helps you charge the ball and it helps you get a little bit extra on your throws.

In playing the outfield, there is one rule that must be followed. Be aggressive. If you're going to worry about hitting walls or running

ONE KNEE. In the outfield, when a ground ball is hit your way and you don't have to make a hurried throw, go down to one knee and make sure the ball doesn't get past you, allowing the batter extra bases. (Photo by Fred Straub)

into someone, you don't belong in the outfield. You have to be daring. You have to challenge fences, make diving attempts. Go after the ball even though you know an infielder or another outfielder is also closing in.

Collisions in the outfield can be avoided. Remember, the center fielder is the man in charge of the outfield. He is the captain, so to speak, the man who makes all the calls. He's the one who can cover the most ground, so he is the one who makes the calls.

If all questionable calls are made by the center fielder, there should never be a collision. A ball hit in the alley in left-center, for example, is the center fielder's ball unless the left fielder hears him holler, "You get it. Yours."

One of the things you try to learn when playing the outfield is the range of the man who plays alongside you. That comes from playing with the man and knowing where he is when the ball is hit. If you know his range, you know which balls he will get to and which he won't.

Always, however, start after the ball as if you are going to catch it. Go until you are called off or until you call for the ball yourself.

On the pop flies in between an infielder and an outfielder, the call belongs to the outfielder. He has the play in front of him.

The infielder, in fact, should never call for the ball. If he can get it, he should make a motion with his arms to let the outfielder know he wants the ball. Then it is up to the oufielder to shout, "Yours. You get it." If the infielder hears the outfielder shout, "I got it," he'd better get out of the way.

Communication is vital. There is absolutely no excuse for players running into one another and letting a ball that should be an out become a base hit.

When catching the ball, two things must be remembered. Whenever possible, use both hands. This is not so much to keep from dropping the ball—today's gloves normally will see to it that you don't drop the ball. It is, instead an aid in getting rid of the ball quickly. If your throwing hand is right there to take the ball out of the glove, you will be able to throw faster than if you have to bring the hand up from your side and into the glove.

The other thing to remember is to catch the ball where you can get

ONE-HAND PICKUP. When you have to make a throw from the outfield (like on a single with a runner at second base), you rush in hard and scoop the ball up with your glove. Notice the concentration on the ball in the first picture. Without wasting a step you come quickly into the throwing position and let go on a low line, aiming at the cutoff man. (Photos by Fred Straub)

rid of it fastest. If you're a right-handed thrower, you don't want to have to reach way out to your left to catch the ball. You want to catch it right about at chin level, out front of your body so you merely remove the ball from your glove and throw.

Willie Mays, of course, was famous for his basket catch, grabbing the ball at his waist. However, when he had to make a throw, he either caught the ball in the orthodox manner or he made the basket catch high, about shoulder level.

I have my own style of catching fly balls. I snap them out of the air. However, if you watch closely, I always use two hands when I do this and I don't do it when I have to throw the ball.

THROWING THE BALL

Throwing from the outfield is just as important as being able to catch a fly ball. You can cut down runs, hold runners from taking extra bases, and even set up outs at a different base.

The throw is directly overhand. This allows the ball to have the proper backspin and to bounce straight and true. Nothing can make you madder than to make what seems to be a perfect throw to the plate and have the ball take a crazy bounce off to one side or the other.

The idea is to field the ball and get rid of it as quickly as possible. That means you have to know where you are going to throw the ball before it is hit. It means that while you are standing in the outfield between pitches, your mind is always working.

"There's a runner on second and one out," you think. "He's not a particularly fast runner. I can go home on a one-hopper right at me. If the ball is hit way to my left or right, I'll probably have to go to second base with the ball."

Always think of what you are going to do so that you can react to the situation as soon as it happens. The one thing you don't want to do is waste time out there.

One way to speed up your throw is to cut down on the number of steps you take before you throw the ball. You catch the ball off your left foot. Then you take a little crow hop—a half-step or so—and come out throwing.

I try to get rid of the ball faster than most guys and throw more accurately because I don't have the strong arm that a lot of outfielders have in the big leagues. A strong arm isn't worth anything if the throw is off-line.

When throwing, keep the ball down. No rainbow throws. The idea is to hit the cutoff man. When throwing to the plate, there will be a cutoff man in the middle of the diamond, directly in line with your throw. You throw the ball on a low line, trying to reach the cutoff man chest-high. If the ball is let through, it will take one hop to the plate. If not, he will cut it off and possibly nail the runner trying for second base after a single.

Remember always to charge the ball. Charging the ball will get you to it quicker and will give you momentum to add strength to your throw.

And always get down on the ball when it is a base hit to the outfield. If no one is on base, go to one knee in front of the ball to make sure it doesn't get through. If the ball gets past you in the outfield, there's no telling how far the runner can go.

PLAYING THE BALL

Judging a fly ball comes naturally. There are some people who just can't do it and, needless to say, these people have no business playing the outfield.

Most people can judge a fly ball. However, you may be having trouble with a certain kind of fly. Maybe it's the ball over your head. Get someone to hit you fungos and concentrate on making that kind of catch. You can improve with work.

The toughest ball to judge is the line drive right at you. You just don't know what the ball will do. It can sink, take off, slide, sail, or even come out like a knuckleball. On this type of ball, you just wait until you see what it is doing, then react. You must stay with it.

On the ball hit over your head, you turn and go to the spot where it is going to land. You get there as quickly as you can, turn, and find the ball as it is coming down. This is almost all totally instinct. Once again, there are some people who can't do it. They have to watch the

I GOT IT. After having called for the fly ball, you set yourself under it and always watch it right into the glove. Catch it up above the head and use two hands. That will allow you to throw the ball more quickly. (Photos by Fred Straub)

ball all the way. There's nothing wrong with that, except that you can't run quite as fast watching the ball as you can if you just turn and run to the spot where the ball will fall.

Practice will help you in judging balls. You have to be able to tell by the crack of the bat how hard a ball is hit. A lot of outfielders will be fooled by a big swing while the hitter hits the ball off his fists. They will start back, thinking the ball was hit hard. Then the ball will fall in front of them for a single. You can tell, though, by the crack of the bat how hard it is hit and you won't be fooled.

There is one rule that will help you judge balls. A left-hander's ball hit toward left field will slice toward the left-field line. If he pulls it, it will hook toward the right-field line. It works exactly the opposite way with a right-handed hitter.

LITTLE THINGS COUNT

There may be something that looks worse on a baseball field than an

outfielder who just stands around and watches a play, but I don't know what it could be. Believe it or not, an outfielder should be doing something on every play.

Every time the ball is hit, the outfielder should be moving somewhere. Maybe he goes to back up a base or a teammate, but he should do something. You can accomplish nothing by standing still in the outfield watching a play.

If you are the left fielder and there is a single to right, move to help back up second base. If there is a single to center, move to back up the center fielder. If the ball gets by him, you will be there to keep the runner from going all the way around the bases.

It might be a one-in-a-million shot, but it might save you a ball game and one game could make the difference between winning and losing the championship.

There are other little things that must be practiced. Practice flipping down your sunglasses so that it comes naturally when a ball is hit up into the sun. I remember in the 1972 playoffs, the Pirates sent Rennie Stennett to play left field in Riverfront Stadium against us. He had a horrible time with the sun. I can sympathize with him because I know what he was going through. But Stennett was an infielder trying to play left field. He hadn't practiced catching the fly balls into the sun.

If you don't have flip-down sunglasses, learn how to shade your eyes from the sun with your glove. Work on it, because you are going to have numerous balls hit into the sun and nothing is more embarrassing or more costly than a routine fly that is lost in the sun and falls for a double.

THE RELAYS

There is one play from the outfield that truly requires a great deal of hard work, but that pays off game after game and season after season. That is the relay.

Normally, on balls hit to the right of second base, it is the second baseman's job to go out and handle the relay. On balls hit to the left of second base, it is the shortstop who handles the relay. The Cincinnati Reds don't operate quite that way. Because Joe Morgan, our second baseman, has a weaker arm than Davey Concepcion, our shortstop, it is Concepcion's job to handle all relays, which means he really has to hustle from shortstop on balls hit to right-center or into the right field corner.

The outfielder's responsibility is to get to the ball as quickly as possible and hit the relay man with the throw. He knows where the relay man is because he has worked on the play time and time again with the relay man. The infielder will go out as far as the strength of his arm permits him.

The outfielder then throws to the relay man, who turns and throws to the base in hopes of getting the runner, whether it be a man trying to score from first on a double or a man trying to make third on a triple.

The play, when executed properly, is as thrilling a play as there is in baseball. In fact, the 1974 World Series was decided on a relay when Bill Buckner of the Dodgers tried to take three bases against Oakland, only to have Reggie Jackson relay to Dick Green, who threw Buckner out by a hair at third base, saving the game and the world championship.

chapter eight

When you stop and think for a moment of your picture of a first baseman, many things come to mind. He is big and strong, a good hitter with power. He is usually left-handed. In the field, while not fast, he usually has grace and quick feet.

Some of the most famous players in the history of the game were first basemen, and many of them fit this mold. There were Lou Gehrig, Jimmy Foxx, Hank Greenberg, Johnny Mize, and Bill Terry.

Modern-day baseball has added to the list with the likes of Willie McCovey, Tony Perez, Lee May, Dick Allen, John Mayberry, Boog Powell, and Steve Garvey, who won the National League's Most Valuable Player award in 1974.

First base normally is the position awarded the man who can hit

playing first base

the ball hard, but lacks the speed of foot or the arm of an outfielder.

Size is one of the first things that is looked for in a first baseman. The taller he is, the fewer throws sail over his head. The taller he is, the more he can stretch to take a throw, perhaps saving a low throw from going into the dirt or just nipping a base runner by a half-step.

But size is not all-important. Garvey, after failing to make it at third base because of his erratic throwing arm, found a home at first even though he is anything but a physical giant. His quick, sure hands and fast feet have made him outstanding at the position.

The hands are extremely important. The first baseman's prime job is to catch throws and put runners out. Therefore, he must be able to go into the dirt to dig out a throw. He must save bad throws from getting past him, allowing runners to take extra bases.

Ideally, the first baseman is left-handed. The reason for this is that most of his throws are to his right. The southpaw can make this play quicker than a right-hander because he doesn't have to turn his body. He merely catches the ball and throws to second or third.

But if you are right-handed, don't fret. There have been many good right-handed first basemen, including Gil Hodges of the old Brooklyn Dodgers, considered the best modern-day first baseman in the game.

POSITIONING

With no one on base the first baseman normally plays behind the bag. His responsibility is twofold. He must cover as much ground as possible, especially to his right. That is another advantage a left-hander has, because his glove is on that side.

The farther he can range to the right, the more the second baseman can cheat toward second and, therefore, take away some of the many base hits that go through the middle.

The first baseman's positioning changes when a runner is on first base. Now he must hold the runner on. The proper position here is to take the inside corner of the base. The first baseman crouches slightly and he holds his glove out, giving the pitcher a target for a pick-off throw.

If the pitcher tries a pick-off, the first baseman catches the ball and moves his glove down to the base. A runner who comes back in standing up should be tagged on his ankle. Don't get in the habit of whipping the glove around high, because most of the time, the man will be diving back in and the tag must be low.

If the pitcher goes to the plate, the first baseman comes off the base quickly toward second, giving him a chance to cover as much ground as possible.

With runners on first and second, the first baseman normally will play behind the runner. He stations himself close enough to the base so the runner can't take too long a lead, yet far enough off so he can cover ground on balls hit his way.

In a bunt situation, with no one on first base, the first baseman

GO AFTER THE BALL. When playing first base, remember you aren't anchored to the bag. If the throw is bad, go and get it. (Photo by Fred Straub)

plays up in front of the base on the grass. As the pitcher delivers, he charges full-speed to field the bunt. With a man on first, he will hold the runner on the base, then charge as the ball is pitched.

Always the first baseman must be alert for a pick-off throw from the pitcher with a runner at first. There is no sign here. If the pitcher feels he can get the runner, he will use his best move and throw quickly. The first baseman can't be fooled or asleep at his position. He must be ready to make the tag.

The pick-off play from the catcher is often on a sign given by the catcher. Here the first baseman will wander off the bag with the

THE STRETCH. The first baseman can make an out on a close play by stretching off the bag. The foot is not set on top of the base but is braced against the inside. This allows you to stretch that much farther and keeps you from being stepped on by the runner. On plays that will be close, go out as far as you can go and always watch the ball right into the glove. (Photo by Fred Straub)

pitch, but not as far as if there were no pick-off on, then scoot back just as the ball is being caught by the catcher, who fires to first.

TAKING THE THROW

The Number 1 thing a first baseman must think about when the ball is hit on the ground in the infield is to get to the base as quickly as possible. The quicker he gets there, the quicker he can set himself to take the throw.

He finds the base with his feet, both heels touching the base. He faces the infielder who has fielded the ball. In this position, he can shift to receive the throw. This is where the quick feet come in.

If the throw is to the right, he will shift so his left foot is on the base and he stretches out with his right. If it is to the left, he allows the right foot to remain on the base and stretches out with the left leg.

The first baseman never crosses over with his legs to catch the ball. That leaves him off balance and cuts down on the distance he can reach for the ball. Baseball is a game of inches and he must get every inch out of his stretch that is possible.

Never stand on the base to take a throw. Catch it and come off the bag so that there is no contact with the runner.

Perhaps the most important play the first baseman makes is catching low throws in the dirt. He can't be afraid of the ball and turn his head. He must watch the throw all the way into his glove. And, he must go down after the ball. Often the first baseman, using that big mitt, will come up with the ball and a glove full of dirt at the same time.

One thing a first baseman must remember is that he doesn't hold the base at all costs. If the throw is too far off the base for him to reach, he must go after it. He doesn't want the ball getting past him.

The throw to the inside that pulls the fielder off the base doesn't necessarily mean the runner will be safe. The first baseman goes after the ball, catches it, and then tries to tag the runner. It is surprising how many runners are put out this way, because normally there's no way they can be tagged if they slide. Yes, you can slide into first base.

MAKING THE DOUBLE PLAY

One of the toughest plays the first baseman has is the first-to-second-to-first double play. It almost always starts with him holding a runner on base, moving to his right to field a ground ball.

Once the grounder is fielded, he must make a throw to second that is one of the toughest in baseball. He must time it perfectly, trying to hit the shortstop about chest-high just as he gets to second base.

But there is always the problem of the base runner being in the way. The throw either has to be lofted over the runner's head or must

HOLDING THE RUN-
NER ON. When there's
a runner on first, the
first baseman takes a
position on the inside
corner of the bag and
gives the pitcher a tar-
get to throw at on a
pick-off. This is the way
you station yourself as
the pitcher stretches.
(Photo by Fred Straub)

be thrown to the infield or outfield side of the bag to avoid hitting the man in the back. The throw from the first baseman is the most important one. He must make sure of one out.

Most of the time, the first baseman can't return to the base to take the throw. If he can't, he has to get out of the way of the shortstop, who will be throwing to the pitcher covering first.

This play takes tremendous timing and can only be accomplished with a great deal of practice. You see it performed less in the big leagues than any other type of double play.

TEAMWORK WITH THE PITCHER

On all ground balls to the right side of the infield, it is the pitcher's responsibility to break toward first base. If the first baseman fields the ball and can make the play himself, he will wave the pitcher off. He does this by waving his arms and shouting, "I'll take it."

If he can't get to the base in time, he lets the pitcher come over and cover the base. The pitcher does not run straight at the base. Instead, he runs to the inside of the baseline about 10 feet in front of the base, turns, and comes down the line to accept the throw.

The throw is a soft one from the first baseman. If possible, he flips it underhand, beginning by holding the ball out in front so the pitcher can see it. He tries to hit the pitcher, just before he gets to the base, about chest-high.

If he's too far from the base to throw underhand, he will make a soft overhand throw. Always, however, make sure the ball is clearly visible to the pitcher, who has a tough enough job coming over, catching the ball on the run and finding the base to step on for the out.

Often the first baseman will go for balls to his right that are fielded by the second baseman. The first baseman can't get back to the base here, so again it is the pitcher's responsibility to cover. This is why on all balls hit to the right side, the pitcher must break for the base. I can't tell you how hard the Cincinnati Reds work on this play in spring training. It is a play that costs an unschooled team two or three games a year, when the pitchers forget to cover first base on balls hit to the right side of the infield.

PLAYING THE BUNT

The first baseman always fields bunts as quickly as possible, charging hard and not worrying about the batter swinging. He must watch the ball all the way into his glove, never fielding the ball barehanded unless he is left-handed and has to make a tremendously quick throw to third.

Even then it is best not to throw the ball, as a bad throw will lead to a run.

The first baseman listens for the call of the catcher, who is in charge on the bunt play because the play is in front of him. He will direct the first baseman where to throw the ball.

If he calls for the throw to go to first base, the fielder catches the ball, pivots and throws to the second baseman covering the base. The throw must be on the inside of the diamond and, once again, up around the chest, where the man can see the ball.

If the call is for a throw to second, the right-handed first baseman pivots and throws hard—but carefully—to the shortstop covering the base. Again the throw should be to the inside and about chest-high.

The throw to third base should be like the others, performed quickly and with a hard, accurate throw that the man can handle.

Cutting down the lead runner on a sacrifice can be a big play in any ball game, but the thing to remember is to make sure you get an out. If the call is for a throw to second base and you bobble the ball, automatically you throw to first and make sure of one out.

chapter nine

If you truly want to learn to play third base, I have one suggestion for you. Go out and get yourself a copy of the 1970 World Series film. That's the one where the Cincinnati Reds met the Baltimore Orioles.

Brooks Robinson put on in that series the greatest one-man fielding show I have ever seen in my life. He robbed Lee May, then with the Reds, so often that May dubbed Brooks with a nickname. "Hoover," he called him. The reason? "Because he's like a vacuum cleaner down there," said May. "Everything hit his way, he sucks up."

Brooks made every play possible and some that weren't possible. He actually dived into foul territory to grab a hot line drive. He dived to his left to rob Johnny Bench of a sure hit.

playing third base

He came in and barehanded a bunt and made an impossible throw to nail the runner at first base.

What was so impressive, though, was that he did all this after having made an error on the first ball hit to him in the World Series. A lot of lesser players would have hung their head and sulked for the full series. But not Brooks. He sucked in his gut and came back.

There is a lesson there. Don't, no matter what position you play, let an error bother you. Once it happens, it's over. There's nothing you can do about it. You just go on and start thinking of the game you are playing and what you can do to help your team. After the game, you may want to practice the kind of play you messed up. But during the game, always keep your head clear. Forget about any failures and think positively, just as Brooks Robinson did.

He went on, after the error on that first ball, to win the car that goes to the Most Valuable Player in the Series. After he won it, I said, "If I knew he wanted that car so bad, I'd have bought it for him myself." I would have, too.

The general impression is that the third baseman has an easier time on defense than the first baseman, but that is not necessarily true.

They don't call it the hot corner for nothing. The position calls for extremely quick reflexes, a strong, accurate arm, and a tremendous amount of courage. Speed is not required at the position. Brooks Robinson is probably the best there has ever been at third base, but he is not a fast runner.

Quickness, rather than speed, is the Number 1 asset a third baseman has. He has to be able to react to hard-hit balls and make the play without thinking.

One of the beauties of the position is that almost everything is hit hard. That means normally the third baseman has time on throws. It also means that he doesn't always have to field the ball cleanly.

The first thing a third baseman thinks of as a ball rockets his way is not to let it get past him. He can drop to one knee, slap at it, take it in his chest. If he keeps the ball in front of him, he still has plenty of time to pick the ball up and throw the runner out.

Pepper Martin of the old St. Louis Cardinals used to play most of the ground balls off his chest, or so they tell me. It is, if possible, better to catch the ball. But sometimes that isn't possible and this is where courage comes in. You must knock the baseball down some way.

COVERING THE BUNT

There is one play that is an absolute must for the third baseman. He must be able to play the bunt. It is the toughest play he makes and the most important.

The play that is especially trying is the sacrifice bunt with runners on first and second. What do you do, charge the bunt and leave third base unguarded, or cover third?

One of the keys is how much ground the pitcher can cover. The pitcher's assignment on the bunt in this situation is to break toward the third-base line. The third baseman must learn just how much ground the pitcher can cover because he has an almost instantaneous decision to make.

Making this play correctly takes a great deal of concentration. The fielder has to decide right away what he is going to do and, when he makes his decision, he must live with it.

If he feels the pitcher will get the ball and covers the base, the pitcher had better be able to get the ball. If not, it's a hit. And if he charges and the pitcher fields the ball, wheels and throws to third . . . well, all those runs may score while the two fielders stand around helplessly.

The third baseman, having decided to cover third base, will wait for the throw from the pitcher, catcher, or first baseman, whoever fielded the bunt. He will take it just as if he were a first baseman, stretching for the ball on the force out. If there is only a runner on second and no force, the third baseman must straddle the bag and make the tag.

Should the third baseman come in to field the bunt, he must remember only one thing. Make sure of getting one out. Unless it is absolutely necessary, the ball should be fielded with the glove.

Often, however, this is impossible. Then the third baseman will come in on the dead run, try to scoop the ball with his bare hand, and in one motion throw to first base. It is such a tough play to execute properly that often it is better not to throw the ball at all. A wild throw could allow two runs to score.

There is one trick play that, on occasion, may be tried. With a slower runner at first with men on first and second, the third baseman may look for a ball that is bunted too hard. If he gets one like that, his best play may be to throw the ball to the shortstop covering second base. The runner on first, thinking the play will be either at third or first, may not be hustling and get caught with his pants down.

THE DOUBLE PLAY

You don't see many third-to-second-to-first double plays during the

SLOW-HIT BALL. The toughest play the third baseman has to make is the topped roller or bunt that he must barehand. Only barehand the ball when no other way exists to make the play. The idea is to catch the ball off the front foot and come up throwing as quickly as possible. Be careful with the throw, though. If you doubt you can make the play, don't throw. (Photos by Fred Straub)

96

course of a season. By the same token, though, you don't see many of those double plays missed when the opportunity presents itself.

The reason is that most often, the ball is hit sharply to the third baseman, giving him time to make a good throw and start the DP.

The throw should be on the inside part of second base, about shoulder-high. This way, the second baseman can get rid of the ball quickly and be able to nail the man running for first.

Once again, make sure of that first throw on the double play. It has to be a good one to allow the double play to be made and, if nothing else, it has to be certain to retire the front runner.

POSITIONING

Normally, the third baseman will play about even with the bag, eight

THROWING FROM THIRD. The third baseman's throw, as shown here, is directly overhand in most instances, with a stride in the direction in which he is throwing. The eyes are glued to the target. Usually, playing third, the ball will be hit hard enough that you won't have to hurry, so make sure the throw is good. (Photo by Fred Straub)

or nine feet off the foul line. If the hitter is a strong right-handed pull hitter, the third baseman will be deeper, five or six feet behind the base and over toward the line. On left-handed pull hitters, he will be deeper than normal and way over toward second base.

If the batter has a tendency to bunt, the third baseman will cheat up on the infield grass.

One thing the third baseman should always remember is the game situation. If his team is nursing a one- or two-run lead in the eighth or ninth inning, he will hug the foul line. No fair ball should be able to get between him and the line. That's a double. You take away the extra base hit. Make the batter hit the ball to your left.

chapter ten

In 1963 I surprised just about all of baseball when I jumped from Macon, Georgia, to the big leagues, beating out Don Blasingame, a veteran of the Reds' 1961 pennant year. My position at the time was second base.

I never won a Gold Glove at second base, but I could handle the position adequately. As a second baseman, I was named the league's Rookie of the Year, so I couldn't have been doing all that much wrong.

Second base is one of the most crucial positions on the baseball field. It is, perhaps, the hardest to play because of the many different and difficult duties the second baseman must perform.

Infield positions in many ways are similar. The main skills are quickness, good hands, and an accurate throwing arm. You catch a

playing second base

ground ball by watching it all the way into the glove and charging the ball. Nearly always, you come in on the baseball, trying to play it and not letting it play you.

The idea is to catch the ball on an in-between hop. You don't want to short-hop the ball—catch it just after it bounced—and you don't want to catch the ball just before it hits the ground. In the middle of the hop—that's just where you should catch the ball.

The one thing you want to remember when catching a ground ball is to keep your glove as low as you can get it. I've seen shortstops come up with a handful of dirt after fielding a grounder. If you are down and the ball takes a bad hop up, you can adjust. For some reason, if your glove is up and the ball darts down, you can't make the same adjustment quickly enough to catch the ball.

INFIELD STANCE. The proper stance in the infield is to be crouched over, feet about shoulder-width apart, up on the balls of the feet. The hands are off the knees, ready to react quickly. The weight is evenly distributed, ready to go in any direction. (Photo by Fred Straub)

Bad hops are going to happen. There's not a thing on earth you can do about them. That's why you try to field the ball directly in front of you. The hop then may come up and hit you in the shoulder or chest and fall where you can still throw the runner out.

Throwing the ball in the infield is similar to throwing from the outfield. The grip is across the seams of the ball. That will keep the ball from sailing to either side. The throw in should be firm, but not overpowering. It has to be handled by other people.

The second baseman's throw is normally a sidearm flip. The shortstop's throw is more three-quarters and the third baseman throws overhand. All throws should be at the letters.

Fielding really isn't as tough as some people make it out to be. I believe you can make a person into a good fielder if he has any kind of athletic ability. Once you convince him to get in front of the ground balls, look them into his glove, keep on the balls of his feet with his knees flexed, and catch the ball with his hands relaxed, it just isn't all that hard.

MAKING THE DOUBLE PLAY

The most important play in baseball is the double play and, in most cases, the most important man in the double play is the second baseman. He must combine quick feet with courage and add an accurate arm when making the pivot.

It isn't easy. There is a base runner bearing down on you and he's intent on knocking you somewhere into left field. You can't even see him. More second basemen are ruined by a fear of the runner than by anything else.

There are three or four different ways of turning the double play as a pivot man. How you make the play will depend on the first throw, the one that comes from the shortstop or third baseman.

In the double play situation, the second baseman "cheats" a little. He will play a bit more shallow and maybe a step or two closer to second base. It is vital that the second baseman break as soon as the ball is hit on the ground so that he can establish position at the bag before the throw gets there.

CATCHING A GROUNDER. The proper stance as you await a ground ball is demonstrated here. The hands are relaxed and all concentration is on the bouncing ball. Notice how you stay in front of the ball and come up throwing. (Photos by Fred Straub)

THE DRAG DOUBLE PLAY. On this double play the second baseman merely drags his foot across second base as he receives the ball from the shortstop or third baseman. He then goes down the line and makes the throw. Usually this is when the second baseman has a bit of time, because he'll wind up having to leap over the sliding runner. (Photos by Fred Straub)

The idea is to get to the base as quickly as possible, with the base positioned between the two feet. From this position, the second baseman can move in any direction, depending on the throw.

The first type of pivot comes with the perfect throw, about letter high and right out in front of the second baseman. This is the crossover pivot.

On this type of pivot, the second baseman drags his left or right foot across the base, moving to the infield side of the bag. As he does, he pivots, steps, and throws to first.

Sometimes it is more comfortable on the good throw to just touch the base with either foot, then back off to the outfield side. The only problem with this type of pivot is that it makes it harder to get as much on the throw to first.

If the throw is to the inside part of the base, the second baseman uses a different pivot. He comes across the bag, sliding his right foot across. As he does, he moves into the infield and throws to first.

Should the throw be to the outside part of the base, the second baseman hits the bag with his left foot and backs off. The most

important thing to remember is to make sure you get one out. If there is doubt about getting two and the throw is especially tough, it is best to hold the ball and settle for the force of the lead runner rather than to rush a wild throw and have the batter wind up at second or third.

The idea of moving off the base after catching the ball is to make sure you avoid being hit by the runner. If he gets you when you have moved out of the base path, it is supposed to be called interference by the umpire and the batter is ruled automatically out.

There are ways to make sure you don't get hit by a runner. Some men gain the reputation of sliding late and hard. You can get them down in a hurry with a low, sidearm throw to first. They either slide or take it between the eyes. Most guys would rather slide. Most of the time, though, the throw on the double play is three-quarters.

A second baseman, by necessity, must use a small glove. It allows him to get the ball out in a hurry on the double play. Joe Morgan, the Reds' second baseman, uses about the smallest glove in the major leagues, not a whole lot bigger than my young son's glove.

105

BACK-OFF DOUBLE PLAY.
One way to make the double play is to come to the base, receive the ball, hit the base with the left foot, then back away out of the runner's way. Notice the footwork involved and the quickness with which you get the ball away to first base. (Photos by Fred Straub)

The best double play man I ever saw at making the pivot was Bill Mazeroski, who was the 1960 World Series hero of the Pittsburgh Pirates. He was so quick, they called him "No Hands" because it appeared that the baseball magically changed directions and headed for first base without his ever touching the ball. I'll always appreciate the help he gave me as a rookie, teaching me to make the double play.

The second baseman isn't always the middle man in the double play. Often he has to start the DP and there is an art to this.

The first thing the second baseman must remember is to take the ball out of the glove. It looks super-fancy to field the ball while moving toward the bag and then flip it with the glove hand to the shortstop. This, however, is a dangerous play, and the most important thing always is to make sure of that first throw.

Two things can happen when you try this kind of play. First, the ball can get caught up in the glove and go wild. That means everyone is safe; the double play ball the pitcher wanted is totally wasted. The other thing is that the shortstop might not be able to see the ball

106

coming out of the glove. That ruins the timing of the play and almost certainly will ruin the chances of getting two.

So it is most important, even on balls hit toward the bag, to take the ball out of the glove, show it to the shortstop, and make an underhand flip.

The underhand throw should come on all throws of less than 10 feet and it is performed as the second baseman steps directly toward the shortstop.

On balls 10 to 15 feet from the base, the second baseman pivots with only the top half of the body, making a three-quarter throw.

On balls hit to the second baseman's left that he must reach for and catch on the run, he will pivot completely around toward the outfield and make a firm throw. The idea on this play is to cut down the lead runner. Most of the time the double play can't be completed.

In close to the bag, the second baseman should perfect a back-handed flip. This is used on slowly hit balls toward the base to save time. It is an important part of the second baseman's repertoire and one of the few things that can be practiced at home, using the backhanded flip into a pillow.

ANOTHER TOUGH PLAY

Here's a play that can drive second basemen loony. Runner on first, no one out. Normally, he cheats up and toward second base for the possible double play. Now, however, the pitcher is batting. It is a bunt situation and the second baseman is in a quandary. He not only must cover second on a ground ball to short or third, but he must cover first on a bunt.

What the second baseman does here is cheat straight forward and watch the hitter intently. If he squares around to bunt, he breaks for first base. If not, he holds his position and is ready to cover second on the ground ball.

If the batter tricks you, turns around to bunt, and then swings away, give him a gold star. He beat you and there isn't a thing you can do about it. You are moving toward first.

THE STEAL

It is the second baseman's job, in most circumstances, to cover second base on a steal when a right-handed hitter is up, and the shortstop's job to cover when a left-handed hitter is up. Teamwork between the two infielders here is vital. They might shout to each other as to which one is covering or they might devise a set of mouth signs. An open mouth may mean it is the shortstop who covers, a closed mouth the second baseman. The glove is held up to the face to hide the sign from the opposition.

It is necessary to keep the other team from knowing which man is covering to foul up the hit-and-run play. You don't want to tell the offense in advance where the hole will be.

On covering the base, you get there as quickly as possible and straddle the bag. Ideally, you catch the ball and snap it down on the inside part of the base, letting the man slide into the ball.

It is best to put both hands down, holding the ball in the bare hand and protecting it with the glove. You turn the back of the glove toward the runner to protect your meat hand.

Don't make a sweep tag. It may look good, but you might miss the runner. Just get the glove down in front of the base and let the man slide into it. It is very seldom that you see a man get spiked.

CATCHING POP-UPS

On pop flies down the line and behind first, the second baseman must take charge, just as the shortstop will do with the third baseman on pop flies down the left-field line.

Normally, the second baseman has a better angle to catch the foul pop than the first baseman and should handle the ball if he can get there easily.

One thing to remember on this play is to stay alert after catching the ball with a runner on base. That man can tag up and advance.

You might recall the play in the 1972 World Series. John (Blue Moon) Odom was pinch-running at third base when a foul fly was lofted behind first.

Joe Morgan went over, caught the ball, turned, and fired home. Odom tagged up and tried to score, barely being nipped by Morgan's alert play. It saved a one-run victory for the Reds and forced the series to seven games.

chapter eleven

It is difficult to separate the shortstop and second baseman in any discussion of how to play the game. They go together like love and marriage. Forever they have been called the keystone combination and, even today, you hear people talking about "Tinker-to-Evers-to-Chance," the double play combination of the Chicago Cubs in the early 1900s made famous in poetry.

Because both men patrol the area through the middle, because they work together so much on double plays, because their duties are so similar, they are tough to separate.

I know when I was in the minor leagues as a second baseman, my shortstop was Tommy Helms, who later was to become an All-Star at second base. Dave Bristol managed us in those early days and made us room together.

playing shortstop

"I want you guys to know everything there is to know about one another," he said. "That way, on the field, you will be able to anticipate the other's moves."

The idea is a good one. Tommy and I became fast friends and it did help our play around second base. Of course, you don't have to go to such extremes. For example, it's said that Johnny Evers and Joe Tinker spent years not talking to one another and still became famous.

One thing I always tried to do before a game was to warm up by playing catch with my shortstop. On the surface, it doesn't appear that this can do much good, but you subconsciously pick up the other fellow's mannerisms and get an idea of how he throws the ball.

Shortstops and second basemen come in all sizes, but it is the one area on the diamond where the little man really has a chance to excel. Phil Rizzuto, the old Yankee great, was just 5′6″ and Freddie Patek of the Kansas City Royals is 5′4″.

Size is one thing you don't look for in an infielder. While you'll take power at these positions—like Joe Morgan, who hits more than 20 homers a year, or Ernie Banks, who hit 500 for his career—it isn't usually required. The defensive importance of the shortstop and second baseman is such that if they are outstanding fielders, they can be weaker at the plate.

In the shortstop, you look for the same things as in the second baseman, with two exceptions. The shortstop must have a strong, accurate arm. The second baseman normally will not have to make a throw of more than 75 feet. The shortstop, however, must make the long throw from the hole. It must be a strong throw and it must be accurate.

The other thing that most baseball men like to see in their shortstop is big hands. This probably started way back in the days of Honus Wagner, considered the greatest shortstop of all time. It's said he had hands like hams and, ever since, that has been one of the things that is looked at.

The shortstop in most cases is the classic athlete. He has speed and quickness and an acrobatic agility to perform miracle plays. He will streak into the hole, backhand a hard grounder, leap, pivot in the air, and throw to second for a force. He will dive to his left for a line drive, then rush a slow bouncer that gets over the mound. He must throw from virtually every position into which the body can bend and the throw must be strong and accurate.

Two things the shortstop and second baseman—at least, the great ones—have is judgment and anticipation. At all times, they know just what they are doing on the field.

On balls hit to the outfield, for example, it is usually the infielders who decide where the throw should go. On balls to the left of second base, the shortstop will go into the outfield and holler directions to the outfielder. He'll tell him to throw home if he has a chance to get the runner, to throw to third, to second, or just to relay the ball into him. The second baseman does the same thing on balls hit to the right side.

TO YOUR LEFT. When moving to your left, you start with a cross-over step and get the glove low to the ground. Once again, watch the ball so you can react to its hops. (Photo by Fred Straub)

How many times have you seen a line drive come screeching off the bat only to go right into the shortstop's glove? It is almost as if he knew where the ball was going to be hit.

Amazingly, often he does know. At least he has a pretty good idea. This is anticipation, and all the great players have it.

The shortstop and second baseman have an advantage in anticipation because they normally station themselves in a position where they can see the catcher's sign to the pitcher. If the call is for an inside pitch, say a fast ball, chances are the ball will be pulled. The fielder then will cheat just a little in that direction.

The next time you attend a big league baseball game, watch the shortstop. As the pitch is thrown, he normally is moving in one direction or another. It may be a very slight movement, but he

TO YOUR RIGHT. On balls hit to your right you won't normally have a chance to get in front of them. You use the crossover step to begin. Again the glove is low and the stretch is full. Concentrate on the baseball. (Photo by Fred Straub)

usually has an idea in his mind of what is about to happen.

Often the shortstop and second baseman will relay the catcher's signs to the other players in the field. That will give them a definite edge, but it also increases the chances of sign stealing by the team at bat.

Perhaps a fast ball is signaled by the shortstop getting into position with his hands on his knees and a breaking ball with the shortstop crouching, his hands dangling in front of him.

THE DOUBLE PLAY

The shortstop has a much easier time of it on the double play than the second baseman, because he is moving in the direction in which he must throw. Everything is in front of him as he comes across covering the base.

The shortstop has a chance to see where the runner is as he bears down on him and also to see the batter moving toward first base. He therefore knows just how much he must hurry on the play.

The shortstop wants the throw to arrive just before he gets to

114

second base. Ideally, it is a shoulder-high throw from the second baseman, a bit to the right so he can get rid of it quickly.

As the shortstop gets to second base, he drags his right foot across the bag. He has all his momentum going toward first base, so he will have no trouble getting a lot of power behind his throw.

In most cases, the runner will be sliding in and the shortstop will have to leap to avoid being dumped. It is best, though, to throw before the leap. That will make the throw more accurate and more powerful.

In starting the double play on a ball hit near second, the shortstop uses an underhand shovel. He doesn't, however, throw the ball from the glove. Always take the ball out of the glove before flipping. Take it in the bare hand and make sure it is held out front so the second baseman can see it all the way.

If the ball is hit close enough to the base, the shortstop can call the second baseman off and take the play himself. He should do this whenever possible, as there is less chance of error.

On balls hit right at the shortstop, his throw to second base normally is sidearm, pivoting toward the base with only the top half of his body.

The toughest play, of course, is the one from the hole. Balls hit to the shortstop's right that are backhanded usually are not double play balls. Think only of getting the force out. If the runner on first is speedy, the shortstop probably will have to leap, pivot in the air and throw to second. If he has time, however, the shortstop should pivot and make the throw toward second without jumping.

TWO TOUGH PLAYS

Perhaps the most important play the shortstop has to make is on the ball in the hole. If he can cover the area to his right extremely well, it virtually assures an airtight defense. The third baseman then can guard the line, cutting down on doubles. The left fielder plays a step or so deeper, not expecting a ball to come through that unguarded area.

And the shortstop himself can cheat a touch toward second base,

THROWING FROM SHORT. In this photo Davey Concepcion, the Reds' shortstop, has just released his throw to first. Notice the concentration and the follow-through, his arm seeming to go in the direction of the throw. In most instances the shortstop's throw must be a hurried one. (Photo by Mark Treitel)

cutting down the area through the middle. That is the hardest area on the diamond to cover.

Whenever possible, the shortstop should get in front of the ball. This is especially true on balls hit to his right. The greatest at doing this was Roy McMillan, the former Reds' shortstop. It was amazing, but even on balls hit way in the hole, he seemed to be charging the ball. That way he was able to get his full body behind the throw.

Sometimes, however, you can't get in front of the baseball and you have to make a backhanded stop on the dead run. Once the ball is caught, momentum will carry the shortstop one more step.

As quickly as possible, though, he plants his right foot, straightens up, and throws directly overhand to first base. This play, executed perfectly, is one of the most exciting to watch in a baseball game because it requires quickness, dexterity, and a strong, accurate throw.

Another tough play for the shortstop occurs when the batter bounces one high off the plate and over the pitcher's mound. As soon as the ball is chopped, the shortstop knows he has to hurry and that he's in for a close play at first base.

As on all slowly hit balls, whenever possible, the ball should be fielded in the glove, not with the bare hand. Once fielded, the shortstop doesn't have time to set himself for the throw. On the run, often with a sidearm motion, he gets rid of the ball as quickly as he can. A wasted fraction of a second in this play can be the difference between an out or a hit.

THE RUNDOWN PLAY

All fielders have to be aware of the proper way to put a runner out in a rundown. It never ceases to amaze me how often this play, which should be a sure out, is botched up.

In 1974, for example, I got caught in a rundown between third and home by the San Francisco Giants. After a couple of throws, the pitcher, covering home plate, started running me back toward third. Seeing he couldn't get me, he threw the ball to third, which by this time was being covered by catcher Dave Rader.

Rader took the ball and started after me. I turned, looked toward home, and saw no one was there. I turned on the afterburner and it was a sight no one could believe. Here I was, heading home, with Rader tagging along behind me. I went into the plate head-first, Rader diving on top of me too late to get me out.

That was an inexcusable sin. In a rundown, every base should be protected and it shouldn't take any more than two throws to put the runner out.

Let's assume for a moment a pick-off at first base by the pitcher. The runner is caught flat-footed and has no way to get back to first, so he breaks for second.

COVERING SECOND. On a steal, the shortstop will come to the front of the base to take the throw from the catcher. If he has time he will make the tag with two hands, the ball in the glove and the back of the glove turned toward the runner. You can see from this photo how close these plays usually are. (Photo by Dick Swaim)

As soon as the first baseman is sure the runner is going toward second, he throws to the second baseman, who is covering the base. Now the second baseman starts running the man back toward first. Always run the man back to the base from which he came, never toward the next base.

The first thing you do as you start to run the man back is take the ball out of the glove and hold it high. You want the man who will receive your throw, if necessary, to see the ball.

Don't pump the ball faking throws as you run. The ball may pop out, allowing the runner to get back safely. The pump fake also has the man who is supposed to catch the throw anticipating a throw each time.

Ideally, the runner, not knowing if there will be a throw or not, can be caught by the man running him back. If not, wait until the last second and throw the ball to the man covering the base.

One rule that must be remembered in the rundown: After

throwing the ball, always cover the base you threw to. In other words, the pitcher picks the man off first, then goes over to cover the bag as the first baseman moves toward second.

When the first baseman throws to second, he moves up and covers that base. And the right fielder has no business just standing out there in the outfield. He should come in to back up a base, as should the center fielder.

The rundown is not as tough a play as some teams make it look. In fact, it is an easy play if executed properly.

THE INFIELD FLY RULE

Before leaving infield play, we might as well go over this rule, which baffles so many people, yet is really quite simple.

The rule merely states that with fewer than two out and runners at first and second—or first, second, and third—any fair pop-up that, in the judgment of the umpire, can be handled by an infielder is an infield fly. The batter is called automatically out and the runners can advance at their own risk. That means the base runners can tag up or can advance (should the infielder drop the ball). They don't, however, have to advance if he drops the ball, since the batter is already out and a force play no longer exists.

This rule was put in as a protection for the runners, not to protect a fielder who may accidentally drop the ball. In baseball's olden days, before the infield fly rule, the runners were at the fielders' mercy.

Say men were at first and second with none out. The batter hit a pop toward third. The runners had to go back to their bases. The third baseman would merely let the ball drop, step on the base, and throw to second for a double play. Both men were forced. With the infield fly rule, this kind of trickery cannot be performed.

chapter twelve

It used to be that the catcher's equipment was called the tools of ignorance. It was figured that anyone who would put all that gear on, climb behind the plate, and take the beating that went along with catching, had to be a dummy.

But look who's laughing now. The catcher, that's who. A guy named Johnny Bench, who happens to be my Cincinnati teammate, came along and the entire image of the catcher was changed. Johnny proved that a catcher can be a complete athlete, a superstar, an idol—and very rich.

There was a time when they took the biggest, strongest, and slowest kid on the block and turned him into the catcher. That was why, for quite a long time, there was a shortage of good catchers in the major leagues.

the catcher

The good athletes were being drawn to all the glamour positions, leaving catching in the hands of lesser players. Take a look at Bench, though, and you'll see what the catcher has to be.

The first physical requirement is strength. The job is no pushover and if you're looking for something that's easy, you might as well skip this chapter. Catching is tough. You continually are crouching, getting up, crouching again. On hot days, wearing all that equipment, your strength will definitely be tested.

In addition, you will wind up taking your share of glancing foul tips and being involved in collisions at the plate.

Remember, we said strength was important, not size. A little, tough guy can catch just as well as a big guy.

The next two assets are quick feet and quick hands. Footwork, which will be discussed later, is vital to the position, as are quick hands.

To catch, a person must own a strong throwing arm. Bench's is one of the best ever and it is an asset that is invaluable to a team. You can't allow the enemy to run the bases at will, and only a rifle-armed catcher can stop it.

Finally, the catcher must be intelligent. Forget all that about the tools of ignorance. It is the catcher who calls all the pitches for the pitcher. He therefore must be able to know what his pitcher throws, what the hitter likes to hit, and the situation.

THE EQUIPMENT

The catcher's glove is the only glove on a baseball team that is unrestricted as to size. Perhaps you've seen some of the catchers who handle knuckleball pitchers like Atlanta's Phil Niekro or the White Sox's Wilbur Wood. They will wear an oversized glove to aid them in their battle to catch the fluttering pitch.

There are really two types of catcher's mitts. The first is the traditional one, which is almost round in shape. This type of glove is fast becoming obsolete in favor of a mitt that is shaped more like a first baseman's mitt.

The pocket in this glove is hinged. The advantage in this type of glove is that it closes almost automatically when the ball hits the pocket. This allows for "one-handed" catching.

It was Bench who made this style of catching popular. It used to be that when you shook hands with a catcher, it was like taking a sack full of walnuts in your hand. That's how many broken fingers catchers used to have.

The reason was that to catch with the round, nonhinged glove, it was necessary to use both hands. This exposed the meat hand to foul tips and there weren't too many catchers who went through an entire season without a broken or split finger.

The introduction of the hinged glove, though, changed all that. The catcher now could handle the pitches with one hand while protecting the meat hand. Seldom do you see broken fingers on foul tips for catchers any more. We'll later go into the art of protecting the bare hand.

In choosing a glove, a catcher should pick one that fits his hand and that isn't too heavy or bulky for him to handle smoothly.

Breaking in the glove correctly is important. The best way to break in any glove is to use it. As often as possible, play catch, concentrating on catching the ball in the pocket.

With a catcher's mitt, usually overstuffed with padding, it won't hurt to hammer in the pocket with a baseball bat. Some catchers even take the glove apart and pull out some of the padding. This is a tricky maneuver and shouldn't be tried unless you are sure you know what you're doing and can get the glove back together again. A glove is too expensive to experiment with.

Saddle soap should be applied to the glove occasionally; it helps keep the leather soft and free of cracks.

One word of warning. Don't leave any glove out in the rain. It can ruin the leather. If, however, you do this, wipe the glove with a towel. Don't ever dry it by putting it near a heater. That will ruin it.

When you are putting the glove away for the winter, it doesn't hurt any to tie a ball in the pocket, helping the glove keep its shape.

A catcher often will use a sponge once his glove is broken in and the padding has shifted. This should be a small, flat sponge that will absorb the shock of the fast ball without making the baseball keep bouncing out of the glove.

The rest of the catcher's gear consists of mask, chest protector, and shin guards. Normally, these are supplied by the team you play for. The only suggestion I have here is to make sure they fit properly and give you adequate protection.

The final piece of equipment a catcher should wear is a plastic cup protector. Never go out to catch without one of these.

GETTING STARTED

The most common error a young catcher just starting out makes is to blink as the ball is coming toward the plate. Blinking is a normal reflex action whenever anything passes in front of the eyes and most catchers find themselves blinking as the batter swings.

123

FLASHING THE SIGN. The sign is given to the pitcher deep back in the catcher's stance. Most important, it is hidden from the peeping eyes of the third base coach and the opposition's bench. (Photo by Fred Straub)

It stands to reason that you can't catch what you can't see. Therefore, you have to control your blinking. Even losing sight of the baseball for just an instant can make the difference between catching the ball or missing it.

To break yourself of the habit of blinking, get yourself a friend or your mother or father. Have them swing a baseball bat back and forth in front of your eyes, six or eight inches away from your head.

Concentrate on not blinking as the bat goes by. Do this over and over, day after day, until you can go behind the plate and catch the game without ever blinking your eyes.

GIVING THE SIGN

One of the catcher's most important duties is to relay to the pitcher the sign that calls for a certain pitch. The catcher must know what's going to be thrown so he can prepare to catch it. Nothing looks worse than a catcher who thought a curve was being thrown only to be crossed up by the pitcher, who whizzes a fast ball by him.

Just as important as giving the sign to your pitcher: you must make sure that the opposition doesn't steal your signs.

The catcher normally will use a finger signal when calling for the pitch. One finger usually is a fast ball, two fingers a curve, three a slider, and five fingers wiggling a change-up.

With a runner at second base, the signs sometimes get more complicated to keep the runner from stealing the pitches. The catcher will use a series of signals, maybe flashing three or four signs. Perhaps the first sign is the one for the pitcher. Maybe it's the second or the third.

Often the first sign will be an indicator. It will tell the pitcher which sign is "live." One finger would say take the next sign. Two fingers would say take the second sign after this. Say two is the indicator and the catcher signals "1-2-1." The pitch would be a curve, two fingers on the first sign after the indicator.

To properly give the sign, the catcher gets down into a deep crouch. His glove is placed on his left knee. This is done to keep the third base coach from stealing a peek at the signs.

The signs then are given back against the right thigh. Make sure the hand is buried in the crotch, but not so low that the fingers extend below the left leg and become visible to the bench.

Never do anything to give away what you are calling. Don't, for example, always look down when calling for a curve and straight ahead for a fast ball. Some smart guy on the other team will pick it up and the opposition will know every pitch your pitcher is going to throw.

Later, we'll go over the proper way to call the game.

THE STANCE

Once the catcher has given the sign to the pitcher, he gets himself into position to catch the ball. He rises out of the deep crouch and balances himself.

The feet should be pointing straight ahead, roughly shoulder-width apart. The weight is evenly balanced on both legs, the catcher up on the balls of his feet. This allows him quick movement in either direction.

The left leg is slightly ahead of the right, making the stance a great deal similar to that of a boxer. The knees are bent, bringing the catcher back down into a crouch.

TWO CATCHING STANCES. There are two basic stances for the catcher. The first is before he is ready to receive the pitch. It is in this stance that he gives the sign to the pitcher. The glove is held at the left knee to shield the sign from the third base coach. The receiving stance has the catcher crouched with his feet about shoulder-width apart, up on the toes ready to move. The glove serves as a target . . .

Most times, the catcher will line up directly behind the plate. The one thing he must do is present a good target to the pitcher. The good square stance behind the plate with the glove held out front gives the pitcher something to shoot for.

If the pitch is to be on the inside, the catcher will set up slightly to the inside and if it is to be to the outside, he will set up on the outside corner of the plate.

The bare hand is held up in front of the catcher, about a foot away from the glove. The hand is closed in a loose fist and turned sideways toward the pitcher. Don't ever open the hand until the ball is in the glove. The only way you will be hurt by a foul tip is if the fingers are extended toward the pitcher.

When catching batting practice, it is best to keep the hand back

126

and the bare fist is loosely clenched to avoid injury from a foul tip. When the ball is on its way, the bare fist is turned slightly so that only the side of the hand away from the thumb is facing in the direction of the mound. (Photos by Fred Straub)

behind you so you can't ever suffer an injury on a foul tip during practice.

FOOTWORK

It is most important with men on base always to be in front of the ball when catching it. This way, a mistake won't result in a passed ball or wild pitch. The catcher will be able to block the ball and keep runners from advancing.

Before even going into the footwork, we should first discuss catching the ball. As it is anywhere else on the field, the ball above the waist should be caught with the glove pointing up and the ball below the waist should be caught with the glove pointing down.

Balls to the catcher's right that he can't get in front of should be backhanded. Reach across the body with a motion that takes the hand over the top. When catching the ball backhanded, the thumb should be pointing toward the ground without twisting the arm.

Now for the footwork. The moves are the same no matter which side the pitch is on. The moves must be made quickly with catlike balance, considering how fast the ball is moving toward the plate.

Always move the foot nearest the ball first. This foot will take a little hop, about a half step in length.

If this doesn't move the catcher in front of the pitch, he then takes a crossover step with the foot farthest from the pitch. The crossover is made to the rear. On an inside pitch to a right-handed hitter, the right leg crosses behind the left.

As soon as that is complete, another step is taken with the foot nearest the ball to regain balance and bring the catcher back into catching position.

The toughest pitches are those that are in the dirt. The catcher must at all costs block this pitch with his body if he can't catch it. It means he can't be afraid to get himself a little dirty.

On pitches that are out front of the plate, the catcher drops to his knees straight forward. If the pitch is a couple of feet in front of the plate, chances are the catcher will let it hit his chest protector.

One thing should always be remembered when blocking balls in the dirt. Remain square with the diamond, facing directly toward the pitcher. That way, if the ball hits the catcher, it will bounce forward. If he has turned his body, the ball will ricochet into foul territory and the runner will advance. If the ball is kept in front of the catcher, the runners will hold their bases.

On pitches into the dirt and off to the side, the catcher uses the footwork previously discussed. The difference is that when he is in position he drops to his knees to keep the ball from going through.

Often, if the base runner is stealing, the catcher will try to catch the low pitch and come up throwing. However, unless he excels at this play, it would be better to go down and block the ball and forget about the runner. If the ball gets by, the runner will make two bases.

PRACTICING YOUR FOOTWORK

The best way to practice your footwork and blocking low pitches is

THE PITCH IN THE DIRT. On the pitch in the dirt the catcher must move to get his body in front of the ball. Bill Plummer of the Reds shows the proper way to do this here. Note that Bill keeps his eye on the ball all the way into his glove. The important thing here, whether you catch the ball or not, is to keep it in front of you so the base runners don't advance. (Photo by Fred Straub)

without a hitter. Get someone to stand 30 feet or so away from you and throw pitches.

Catch him with the full gear on and make sure he throws some pitches in the dirt to your right and to your left. He should do this on purpose, over and over, until you can move in both directions equally well.

You'll take some bumps and bruises handling this practice. But in the long run it will be worth it. You want to be able to react instantly to any situation, any pitch, and keep the baseball from getting past you.

Never, with men on base, just reach for an inside or outside pitch.

It looks lazy and in the long run will cost your team runs and, therefore, victories.

THROWING

Assuming you own a strong throwing arm, which is one of the requirements for being a catcher, the two major things to worry about when throwing are a quick release and accuracy. These two things allow you to throw runners out even if your arm is something less than Johnny Bench's.

There are three throws that concern the catcher: nailing a base stealer, trying to pick a runner off base, and throwing a hitter out on a bunt or tap in front of the plate.

The catcher's throw is different from the throw for any other player on the field. Since accuracy and quickness are most important, he has his own technique.

The ball is held across the seams. The catcher should try on every pitch to grab the ball in this manner. If he works at it, it will come naturally and he won't have to look in his glove to see if he has got the ball properly.

The throw is made directly overhand. The reason is to make sure the ball travels straight and true, never tailing off or sailing.

Instead of reaching far back to throw, the catcher throws right from the ear. The ball is caught, taken out of the glove with the bare

THE CATCHER'S THROW *(right to left).* The catcher's throw must be quick and accurate. After catching the ball with a runner going, the catcher is moving forward immediately, taking only one step with . . .

130

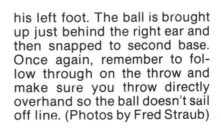

his left foot. The ball is brought up just behind the right ear and then snapped to second base. Once again, remember to follow through on the throw and make sure you throw directly overhand so the ball doesn't sail off line. (Photos by Fred Straub)

131

hand, and brought quickly back to the ear, no farther. That saves time.

On a steal, the catcher is leaning forward as he catches the ball. He takes but one step with his left foot, directly toward the base he is throwing to. Then he fires.

On the steal, the ball should be delivered to the base, arriving about knee high and just to the right of the base. That will allow the man covering to catch the ball and make the tag in one motion.

When the runner is trying to steal third base, the same snap throw is used. However, the footwork has the catcher stepping toward third base. If a right-handed batter is up, the catcher will step behind the batter on his throw to the base.

The pick-off throw to first base, again, is the quick snap pitch from the ear. The ball is caught and the catcher pivots on his right foot, wheeling to the right, stepping, and throwing to the base. Never throw without stepping in the direction in which the throw will go.

FIELDING THE BUNT

One of the most difficult plays the catcher has is on the bunt. It is his job to call the play if he cannot field the ball.

This, of course, requires keen judgment. The catcher must be aware of the speed of the base runners, the jump that runner may have gotten, and the fielding abilities of his own infielder.

On the sacrifice bunt, the most important thing to remember is that you must get one out. If the catcher's call is to throw out the base runner, he'd better be right.

To add to the situation, with a runner on first and a bunt down the third-base line, the catcher has another responsibility. If the third baseman fields the ball, the catcher goes to cover third base as soon as he shouts for the play to be made at first. If he doesn't do this, the base will be left unguarded and the runner can move up two bases on the sacrifice.

As soon as the hitter squares around to bunt, the catcher should be leaning toward the infield. The quicker he can get out after the bunt, the better his chance of nailing the base runner.

FIELDING THE BUNT. The catcher, as quickly as possible, moves out to the ball. If it is rolling, he stops it with his glove. If it has already stopped, he picks it up by scooping it with his bare hand into the glove. Always use the glove when fielding a bunt. And keep your eye on the ball until you have full control of it. (Photo by Fred Straub)

Bunts are never to be fielded with one hand. The idea is to stop the ball from rolling with the glove while sweeping it into the glove with the bare hand.

Once the ball is fielded, the catcher straightens up and steps toward the base he is throwing to. Very seldom will you see the catcher field a bunt and throw all in one motion without straightening up. If the bunt is close enough to the plate for him to field, it will give him enough time to make sure of the throw.

133

THE POP-UP. When the ball is hit in the air, the first thing the catcher does is shed the mask. He doesn't just flip it off. Instead, he takes it off and throws it in the opposite direction from which he is going. Once under the ball, he catches it up above his head and makes sure he uses two hands. Always remember, foul pops will drift back toward home plate. (Photos by Fred Straub)

The throw should always be to the infield side of the base. This is especially important on throws to first base. On throws to first, the catcher has the runner to contend with. The runner, however, isn't allowed to run to the inside of the baseline, so that's where the throw should be.

If the runner is running on the inside of the foul line and is hit with the catcher's throw, he should be called out for interference.

THE FOUL POP

Nothing looks easier than catching a foul pop-up and nothing is more deceiving. This is a play that takes hours of practice and proper technique and it isn't an easy play.

One rule will help the catcher here. Generally, an inside pitch to a right-handed batter will be fouled off to the catcher's right and an outside pitch to the catcher's left. It works just the opposite for a left-handed hitter.

The first thing the catcher must do is spot the ball and make a judgment as to where it will land. This comes from practice.

Another rule to remember is that all foul pops behind the plate drift back toward the playing field because of the spin on the ball.

As soon as the ball is fouled off, the catcher must get rid of his mask. Don't just flip the mask off. Take it off with the bare hand and as soon as you know where the foul is going, throw the mask in the opposite direction. That way, you'll never trip over it, break an ankle, and miss the ball.

As the ball goes up, the catcher should take his eyes off it. If he doesn't, it will look like a twisting, bouncing dot in the sky and will be almost impossible to catch.

Instead, go to the place where the ball will land and pick the baseball up just as it starts down. You'll have time to adjust to any misjudgment on your part as the ball comes down.

The ball should be lined up as if it were going to hit the catcher in the head as it comes down. It should be caught in front of the body, waist high and with both hands.

HANDLING THE PITCHER

Pitchers, believe it or not, are people and, therefore, there are no two

135

of them who are exactly alike. To handle them well, the catcher must be a master at psychology and a student of people.

There are pitchers like Clay Carroll of the Reds who constantly must be pumped up with compliments. When he makes a good pitch, he needs to know it from his catcher.

Some pitchers may lack concentration. The catcher then must constantly keep them in the game. Shout out instructions to this kind of pitcher. Make sure he knows to stretch when a runner is on base. Tell him what to do in a bunt situation. Discuss how he wants to pitch to certain batters. That will get him thinking.

Other pitchers have a tendency to let down when things start going against them. You can almost bet with that type of pitcher, he will give up a hit after one of his teammates commits an error. This kind of pitcher is almost begging for someone to console him.

"Forget about it. Bear down. You've got to get this guy. You can do it," the catcher will instruct.

The catcher must also know the habits of his pitchers. Some pitchers—like Bob Gibson—work best when they work fast. Others need to slow things down. Often a pitcher will begin working too fast. If that happens, the catcher may go out and have a little talk with him to calm him down or he may just take his sweet time getting into a crouch and giving the signal.

The catcher must also know which pitches his pitcher likes to throw and has confidence in. If the pitcher has confidence in his curve, the catcher won't be afraid to call it with the count 3-and-1 or 3-and-2.

Sometimes the pitcher may have confidence in a pitch that isn't working on that particular day. The catcher must make the pitcher aware of this; tell him that some other pitch is working better.

One thing the catcher must always realize: It is the pitcher who must throw the pitch and it is the pitcher who will get the credit if it works or the blame if it fails.

Therefore, the catcher must go along with the pitcher if he shakes off the sign. If the catcher really believes the sign he gave was the one and only pitch to throw, he should go out to the mound and try to convince the pitcher of his thinking.

However, sometimes it's better if the wrong pitch is thrown with confidence than to have the right pitch thrown by a pitcher who wants to throw something else.

The catcher and pitcher must become an entity, a unit. Before every game, the catcher will meet with his pitcher of the day. They will discuss every hitter they will face and decide how they want to pitch to each one.

If this is done, during the game, the catcher and pitcher will be thinking along the same wave lengths and the chances for disagreements will be small.

BLOCKING THE PLATE

One of the most exciting plays in baseball comes when a runner is trying to score and there is a play at the plate.

The catcher's job is to protect the plate with his life and limb. But there's a catch. The rules don't permit the catcher to block off the plate until he has caught the ball. You can't let the runner slide into you, then catch the ball and make the tag. To block the plate, you must have the ball.

On plays at the plate, the catcher should station himself on the infield side of the plate. The left leg should be planted directly in the base path, just in front of the plate so the runner has nowhere to slide other than into the shin guards.

The ball should be caught and the tag applied with both hands. One-handed tags, the play that Bench does better than anyone, should only be used if there is no other way in which to get to the runner. The catcher will use the one-handed tag when he has to leave the plate to catch an off-line throw, diving back in to make the play.

At no time should the catcher block the plate by dropping to his knees. That leaves him exposed to the spikes of the base runner. The shin guards will take care of guarding the plate.

Runners usually will try to slide coming into the plate. On occasion, there is a situation where the runner decides the only way he can score is by running full force into the catcher, trying to jar the ball loose. If a collision can be avoided, it should be. A runner who isn't going to slide is easy to spot and the catcher can wheel out of his way, making the tag as the runner goes past. Don't be fooled, though, and let the man slide under you.

chapter thirteen

I can still recall the first game I ever pitched. I was nine years old at the time, trying out for the Little League. In those days, coaches built their teams by bidding for different players, and they held a tryout to see just who had the ability.

All I know is that when I threw, all the coaches gathered around me. Even then I could throw the baseball very hard. I guess they liked what they saw because the man who got me for his team spent most of his points on me.

I guess I was very fortunate. I had the two qualities you look for in a pitcher, a strong arm and control. I always had them and they came naturally. But I'm not going to tell you that if you don't come by either naturally, you should forget about pitching.

Each quality is necessary. When scouts go out looking at a

pitching
by don gullett

pitcher, they look at his arm and his control. But a guy can pitch and win in the big leagues even if he can't knock over a brick wall with his fast ball. And, if he throws hard, he has a chance even if his control is somewhat shaky.

Recall, if you can, Stu Miller, who pitched in the 1960s for Baltimore and the Giants. He threw the ball at two speeds, slow and slower. But what a pitcher he was. He relied on finesse.

Who should pitch? That's a tough question to answer. You see all different types of pitchers. There are heavy pitchers, like Mickey Lolich of Detroit and Wilbur Wood of Chicago. There are thin pitchers like Tom Hall, who pitched a few years with the Cincinnati Reds and was thin; he was nicknamed "Blade." There are tall pitchers like James Rodney Richard of Houston, who is 6'9", and there are short pitchers, like Fred Norman of the Reds, who is 5′8″.

Whatever your physical assets, you have a chance to pitch. But don't think it comes easy. It takes work and a lot of it. Just being able to throw hard doesn't do it. I know.

When I came up to the big leagues at 18 in 1970, I could throw hard. I was used in relief and threw just about nothing but fast balls. You can get away with it for a while, but before long the hitters catch on. They wait on the fast ball and can handle it.

You have to be able to throw something else to be a success and you have to be able to control what you throw. Work, that's the only way to get there. I can remember the days when I was a kid in Lynn, Kentucky, a little town on the Ohio River.

We played ball every day, and as a youngster, I threw a lot. Scouts today are complaining that kids' arms aren't as strong as they used to be when they are signed because they aren't playing as much ball as they used to.

I know I spent many an hour throwing a baseball when I was young. I'd throw to one of my brothers while the other brother hit. We'd work at least three times a week, often every day. It helped mentally and physically. It helps build up the arm and it helps you work on throwing the ball where you want it.

CONDITIONING

Some people wonder why conditioning is such an important part of pitching. After all, a starting pitcher pitches just once every fourth or fifth day and a relief pitcher, while he might work four or five times a week, doesn't stay very long in a game. But conditioning is vital to success as a pitcher.

No one uses more stress and strain than a pitcher when he performs. He uses every bit of stamina he has to go through a nine-inning game.

If you don't believe it, just try to pitch nine innings in St. Louis with the temperature 90 degrees and the sun beating down on you standing on the artificial surface. Try reaching back for something extra in the eighth inning with a one-run lead, two on, and Reggie

Smith hitting. If you try it, you'll know the pitcher has to be in shape.

When I talk about conditioning, I mean the entire body, not just the arm. I feel that the legs play as big a role in pitching as the arm. You can't pitch without legs and your arm is only as good as your legs. The first thing you must do every year is get your legs in shape. The arm will come later. It takes the arm longer than the legs to get in shape and, until the legs are in shape; you really can't use the arm well.

What you have to do is a lot of running, a lot of the right type of exercising. Your running should be a combination of distance running and sprinting. Early in the year, distance running is probably best because it builds your wind and your stamina. The short sprints keep you strong.

We run with the Cincinnati Reds probably as much or more than any other team in baseball. For example, they tell me Johnny Sain, the pitching coach of the Chicago White Sox, doesn't believe in his pitchers doing a lot of running. I can't go along with the theory at all.

With the Reds once the season starts, we sort of combine distance running with sprints. Every day, we do at least 12 sprints of 50 to 75 yards. What we do is sprint down at a good speed, then jog back. We never really stop running.

It is best to take things slow early in the year, after the long winter's layoff. Worse than underdoing it is overdoing it too early. This is especially true when it comes to throwing the baseball. I've seen a lot of kids come to spring training with a chance to make the team and extend themselves too early. They look good for a while because they are trying so much harder than the veterans. Before long, though, they wind up nursing a sore arm or a pulled muscle. You can't do too much too early.

It's important to remember to loosen up well before you start doing any strenuous work. We do about half an hour of exercises a day with the Reds in spring training right at the start of the day's work. Mostly, this is stretching and bending exercises to loosen the muscles.

We'll touch our toes, right hand to left toe and the opposite. We'll stretch out the groin muscles and do a lot of bending to stretch the back out. A good exercise is to stand with your feet wide apart, lean over your knee and put all your weight on it. Do it with one leg, then the other.

We also have gone into work with the Nautilus. This is used to build strength in the muscles, but we are very careful with it. We want to build strength and not bulk. Bulk hurts a player's ability to move and that's something he can't afford in baseball. If you are going to go into Nautilus training, be sure an expert sets the program up for you.

TAKING CARE OF YOUR ARM

You may not be able to pitch without your legs, but the arm is your most valuable possession as a pitcher. It must be handled with care. Early in the year, it is best not to overwork it. When you get tired from throwing, stop.

During the season, it is best to warm the arm up slowly. Begin by lobbing the ball. You start from just a few feet away from the catcher, progressing back to the 60 feet, 6 inches as the arm gets looser. I work on my fast ball first as I'm loosening up for a game, but I always work in my other pitches. It is important to throw every pitch you have when warming up because you often use different muscles for different pitches and these must be loose.

Once you feel nice and loose, usually after about 15 minutes of throwing, get your warm-up jacket on and wait until you go to the mound.

The normal procedure after pitching a game is to get ice on the arm. That helps keep it from swelling and it helps heal all the broken blood vessels you will have from extending yourself while pitching. Give it a full 15 minutes or more of ice, then take the next day off.

You are normally stiff the day after you pitch a game. The arm is still recovering. Therefore, don't throw one day after you pitch. Relax, enjoy the game. On the second day, you give yourself a good, hard workout, getting all the stiffness out. Take another day off after that and then on the fourth or fifth day, the arm is ready to go again.

I must emphasize one thing. Work out during the off-season, too.

Pitching is a year-round job. If you can throw during the winter, do it. I know as a kid I played football and basketball and that helped me stay in shape, to say nothing of helping my high school team win games in both sports.

EQUIPMENT

The pitcher's glove is bigger than the infielder's or outfielder's. Not because it helps him field any better, but because it helps hide the baseball from the hitter.

A glove nowadays is a big investment and anyone interested in buying one should take his time about it. Go slow and get the right glove for you.

A lot of kids go for a glove because they idolize a player and buy his model even though it isn't the right glove for them. You don't want a glove that is too big for your hand, that is bulky and can't be moved. It should, however, be roomy inside, yet easily handled. Don't buy a glove to grow into. Buy one that fits.

As for the shoes, the most important thing is that they fit, not look pretty. You can buy them with stripes or in colors, but that doesn't mean a thing.

Buying baseball spikes is different from buying regular shoes. You should buy the spikes a half size smaller than your street shoes. They should feel tight. The important thing is that there's no room for your foot to move around inside. That causes blisters and blisters are something that must be avoided.

With the spikes, you'll want a toe plate to keep the shoe from wearing out. Without a toe plate, you'll go through your shoes in a hurry, right where your toe scrapes along the mound as you follow through.

Before you ever pitch in a pair of shoes, break them in well. That means do a lot of running in the shoes to make sure they are form-fitting to your feet. That way, you will avoid blisters.

THE STANCE

The first thing you do before delivering the pitch to the plate is stand on the mound and take the sign from the catcher. This is about the only time you can do nothing wrong when pitching.

There really is no correct way to stand. You stand with one or both feet on the pitching rubber. If you decide you like only one foot on the rubber, the other foot will be to the rear.

The important thing is to be comfortable and to set yourself a stable base from which to work.

I like to have the baseball in my glove when I'm taking my stance and reading the sign. The glove is out in front of me, where I can reach in and grip the ball. The reason I do this is to hide the ball from the hitter and the coaches.

If you hold the ball in your bare hand, you may tip off the pitch. Maybe when throwing the curve, you will show more of the ball in your grip than in throwing the fast ball. A smart coach at third base will notice this and before long, you'll hear him relaying the information to the hitter in the form of a sign. The baseball should be in the glove so you don't have to turn it to grip it correctly. That could lead to tipping the pitch off also.

It is important to find the spot on the rubber from which you pitch best. I'm different from most left-handers in that my pitching is done from the center of the rubber. Most lefties go off to the left-hand side of the rubber and most right-handers pitch from the right. I've tried throwing from the left side, but there's something about it I don't like.

Maybe it's psychological, but whatever it is, I go from the middle. Standing off to the left gives me a different view of the batter and a different view of the strike zone and the ball is coming at a different angle. It's not for me.

You should experiment and find your spot on the rubber. Wherever it is comfortable for you, that's where you pitch from.

As you stand on the rubber, your left foot, if you are left-handed, or your right foot, if you are right-handed, is half on, half off the rubber. The front cleat on the shoe should be in the dirt and the back cleats planted in the rubber.

It is from that position that you read the catcher's sign. Once you agree with the sign, you begin to pitch.

144

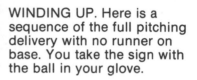

WINDING UP. Here is a
sequence of the full pitching
delivery with no runner on
base. You take the sign with
the ball in your glove.

After getting the sign, reach
in and get a grip on the ball
as you start your motion.

Bring the hands fully up over the head, and then as the hands start down, you start to kick forward. Note as you kick you are concentrating on your target.

146

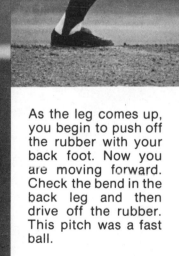

As the leg comes up, you begin to push off the rubber with your back foot. Now you are moving forward. Check the bend in the back leg and then drive off the rubber. This pitch was a fast ball.

147

Just as your front foot hits the ground, you are bringing the ball forward, still concentrating on your target. Now, with all your force moving toward the plate, you have reached the point to deliver the ball. My facial expression tells you how much energy goes into every pitch. After releasing the ball, you follow through fully, the throwing arm almost wrapped around the body. Note the eyes are still on the plate. (Photos by Fred Straub)

THE WINDUP

There really isn't any right way to wind up, which is the motion you use before delivering the pitch, with no one on base or with a runner at third base. All you have to do is watch a few games to see how varied the windup can be.

Juan Marichal used to kick his leg high in the air. Don Larsen used a "no windup" delivery. Luis Tiant does things from a herky-jerky motion.

The important thing is to do what is comfortable and natural to you. Don't copy other pitchers. They have, over the years, developed their own style.

You are standing on the mound, your shoulders square to the plate, the ball in your glove and your foot on the rubber. The first thing you do is reach into the glove and grip the ball. Don't ever start the windup until you have the proper grip.

We will talk about this as if it were for a left-handed pitcher—which I am. A right-hander will do just the opposite.

The first thing you do after having gripped the ball is take a little rock back onto your right foot. This is similar to the forward press in golf. It gets the rhythm of the delivery started and gets your momentum going.

The hands are raised up above the head as you do this, the glove hiding the ball from the hitter.

Now, you begin to move forward. The weight shifts back to the foot on the rubber, the left one for a lefty. At this point, there should be a slight bend in the leg on the rubber. This is to give you the drive you need to make the pitch.

At all times you are keeping your eyes on the spot where you are planning to throw the ball. Don't turn your head or drop it. Keep those eyes glued to the target.

At this point in the delivery, you begin to kick. You swing your rear leg forward, swiveling the hips to get it out front. How high you kick depends on what feels best for you.

As you begin kicking, you also begin probably the most important thing in pitching. You start to drive off the rubber with your back foot.

You move toward the plate, bringing your arm around quickly, and release the ball, then follow through with the arm.

Pitching, you see, is very mechanical, and it's a whole lot more than meets the eye. People come to the ball park and see a guy out there and they think all he has to do is grab a ball and throw it over the plate. Anything else is the truth. There are a million minor things and it takes a lot of work.

Of course, you don't have to worry about all these little things. A couple of times out on the mound and you'll find the mechanics all come without thinking. Only when things aren't going well will you have to sit back and take stock and see just what you are doing wrong.

For example, if you are throwing everything high, chances are the problem stems from keeping the leg on the rubber too stiff. If you're too low with the pitches, you probably are bending the knee too much, causing you to throw low and to lose power.

The most critical time in the delivery is right there as the kicking leg is at its highest point and the rear leg is beginning to drive. That is where it all comes together.

Some pitchers will find it more to their liking to go with a "no windup" delivery. Here they just move right into the motion without bringing their hands over their head and without much of a kick. I don't like this because it makes it too easy for the hitter to see the ball. All he does is follow the pitching arm.

I like to try to be smooth with my delivery, not herky-jerky. Yet, it is important—no matter what delivery you use—to have that rhythm so that it all comes together into a good pitch.

It is important to think about your landing as you pitch. The foot comes down out of the kick and you land on the ball of the foot. By this time, because you have driven off the rubber, your rear foot should be three to six inches in front of the rubber.

You must land at the same spot every time you pitch. You don't shorten your stride one time or lengthen it another. That will louse up your control but good. And, as the foot hits, you soften the landing by bending the knee. You don't ever land stiff-legged. The

FAST BALL. This is the way I grip my fast ball, which is my best pitch and the best pitch for most pitchers. The ball is held across the seams at their widest point, the thumb under the ball. It is released off the tip of the two fingers. (Photo by Fred Straub)

foot that lands should always be pointed in the direction you are throwing.

The release point of the ball has a lot to do with the legs. If the back leg is bending too much, your arm will wind up running behind your body and you will let it go too far back, making the pitch high. If the leg is stiff, the arm will get out front of the body because there is no drive and the pitch will be low.

All this comes from experience and it is something you don't think about when pitching.

THE FOLLOW-THROUGH

Everyone is different. Some guys wind up in the perfect position, with both feet square toward the plate, their glove up ready to field, and looking at the hitter.

When I throw, my leg comes through and I turn almost all the way around, so my back is almost toward the hitter. Jack Billingham of the Reds is the same way. How he follows through all depends on the style of the pitcher. The one important thing is that you *must* have a follow-through. You can't stop the motion of your arm just as you release the ball.

THE FAST BALL

To most pitchers, the Number 1 pitch they throw is the fast ball. Without it, they can start looking for a 9-to-5 job. I'm one of those pitchers.

151

When I first entered the big leagues, being used in relief, I just reared back and let go. Time after time. Sometimes on every pitch. The fast ball was it. I was being called into games in tight spots and had to go with my best pitch. That was the fast ball and I could get away with it because chances were I'd see any given hitter only once a game.

The fast ball, of course, is the most natural pitch for a pitcher to throw. I throw 80% fast balls right now. But I keep cutting that percentage down from those days when I was young and in relief. The more I learn about using other pitches in situations, the more I use them, and that can't do anything but help me.

There are two ways to grip the fast ball. You can grip it across the seams of the baseball or with the seams. Most guys who throw the ball overhand or three-quarters, will grip the ball across the seams. This will give them a "riding" or "rising" fast ball.

It is important that the ball move when it comes to the plate. No matter how hard you throw, a straight fast ball is a bad fast ball. It will be hit. The ball must rise as it comes to the plate, or sink or sail. It must do something.

I like to grip the ball across the seams because I've found the rising fast ball is best for me. You grip the ball at the widest point in the seams with the thumb directly under the ball.

The hand should be firm on the ball, but not too firm. It should feel comfortable in the hand and, most important, it should be gripped up in the fingers, not way back in the hand.

The fast ball is thrown with a natural motion, the ball sliding out of the hand and coming off your index and middle finger at the same time. As the ball is being thrown you snap the wrist to give it the most rotation you can and, therefore, the most hop.

As you are throwing the fast ball, you must get as much drive as possible out of the leg on the rubber. The more effort put into the drive, the faster the ball will move.

The rotation of the fast ball is a backward spin, moving rapidly. This is what will make it hop as it goes toward the plate.

THE CURVE BALL

There was a time when it was popular to theorize that the curve ball

THE CURVE. Here is the way I grip my curve ball. I use the seam under my middle finger to get the ball to rotate. Picture at right shows the way the ball is at the release point. It should roll off the index finger as the wrist is snapped down hard. (Photos by Fred Straub)

was nothing but an optical illusion. If this be so, then I've seen a lot of guys who struck out on optical illusions. Let me tell you right now, you can make a baseball curve and you'd better learn how. Not that you should start when you are eight years old. At a younger age, just work on developing the arm and control. Stay away from the curve because your muscles aren't developed to the point where they are ready for that yet.

At 13 or so, you can start working on the curve ball. And work is just the right word. It doesn't come easily.

The curve ball is one of those pitches that helps separate the good hitters from the bad. It not only comes to the plate at a reasonable speed, but it breaks sharply down and away, if it is a right-handed pitcher throwing to a right-handed hitter, or a left-handed pitcher throwing to a left-handed hitter.

The grip on the curve ball is different from the grip on the fast ball and that's one of the major reasons you start with the ball in your glove rather than in your bare hand. You can see a pitcher changing the grip in his bare hand and that could tip off the curve to the hitter.

What I look for is one of the biggest seams in the baseball. Yes, the seams sometimes differ in size. You are now going to grip the ball with the seams, the middle finger having that biggest seam directly under it. The index finger rests on the cover of the ball.

It is the middle finger that makes for the curve ball, exerting more pressure on the baseball than the index finger. Pulling down on that seam with the middle finger as you release gives the ball its rotation and makes it curve.

To throw the curve, you need a strong wrist. With the wrist, you give a simple pulling action, as if you were reaching and pulling down a window shade. As you do, you snap the wrist down sharply. The ball actually rolls over the top of the index finger, having a downward spin, causing it to break.

When throwing the curve, the knee break of the leg on the rubber is slightly less than that for a fast ball. And, on landing with the foot that is kicking, you will want to bend that knee even more than normal. This will make sure you keep the curve ball down below the hitter's waist.

In throwing the curve, the follow-through becomes very important. If you don't make sure the arm comes all the way through, you will be "quitting" on the curve, a common mistake. That takes rotation away from the ball and makes it come in high. The result is a "hanging" curve ball, about the easiest pitch there is to hit in baseball.

You start throwing the curve ball right if, when the ball is rolling over the index finger and being released, the palm of your hand is facing you—the pitcher—and the back of the hand is pointed toward the hitter.

THE CHANGE-UP

The change-up is one of the best pitches a pitcher can have in his repertoire. It is also one of the most dangerous.

A hitter looking for a change-up and getting one can hit it 12 miles. A hitter not looking for a change-up and getting one can look ridiculous.

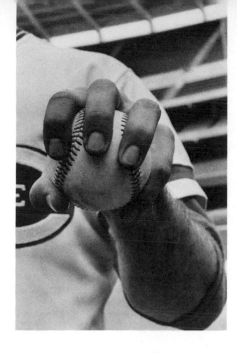

CHANGE-UP. This is one of many ways to throw the change-up. The ball is held with all five fingers and pretty much pushed toward the plate. (Photo by Fred Straub)

The name of the pitch implies exactly what it is. It is a change-of-pace pitch, something that is much slower than the fast ball. Since hitting is all timing, a pitcher tries to throw the hitter's timing off. One way is with the change-up.

It is not an easy pitch to throw. In fact, I spent years working on a change and finally abandoned it to use a fork ball. That will be discussed later.

The most important thing to remember is to use the same motion as you use with the fast ball. The change-up has to look like a fast ball right up until it is released from the hand.

Don't speed up your motion or try to look like you are putting extra effort into the pitch during the windup. That is a tipoff to the hitter, and the hitter who is looking for the change-up is the most dangerous man in the park when one is coming.

You grip the change-up by choking it way back in the hand. While the fast ball and curve are held out in the fingers, the change-up is held back against the palm of the hand. That way, no matter how hard your arm motion, the ball cannot move as fast as a fast ball.

To make sure you have no power, you really break the leg on the rubber. You take as deep a bend as you can going back, almost sit down, but you don't drive out of the crouch as you throw the pitch. That makes it slow and effective.

155

Remember to keep the pitch low, right about at the batter's knees. And don't overuse the pitch. It is good to throw a hitter's timing off, but it is a pitch that must be set up with your hard stuff.

THE SLIDER

The slider is the one pitch that gives the pitcher the advantage. It is, if you prefer, "The Equalizer." It looks like a fast ball. It comes in like a fast ball. It makes the hitter commit himself.

Then, whip, it moves five or six inches. It is the pitch you use for the out and, if thrown correctly, it isn't much strain on the arm.

The slider I use is actually termed "a cut fast ball." All that means is that I throw a fast ball, but it has a rotation something like a top.

The grip is like a fast ball grip. The difference comes in the release. With the fast ball, the hand is straight coming through. With the slider, the hand is turned.

The way to look at the release of the slider is as if you are throwing a football. It is thrown with a spiral-type rotation on the ball.

With the slider, just as you are releasing the ball, the hand turned sideways toward the hitter like a karate chop, you pull down sharply. It's not a snap of the wrist or anything like it. The entire arm is pulled down. This will give it a quick, late break, no more than four to eight inches.

A lot of guys who throw the slider have a bigger break in theirs. That's because, right at the end of the delivery, they snap their wrist violently. This, however, works the muscles in the arm down around the elbow and could cause damage if thrown that way over a long period of time.

The slider has been a big pitch to me. It looks like a fast ball to the hitter and gets to him real fast with that quick break. It is hard to read since there isn't much difference in the rotation between a slider and a fast ball.

If you get the hitter committed, and the ball then slides in on his hands, it will saw his bat off. He's in trouble if he has committed himself because he can't adjust when the ball slides four or eight inches at the last moment.

156

MY TRICK PITCH. Here is the way I grip the fork ball. Note the wide spread in my fingers, brought about by working on the pitch so much. The ball will come to the plate with little rotation. (Photo by Fred Straub)

THE FORK BALL

This is a freak pitch, going right along with the screwball and knuckleball, but it's been a great pitch for me.

To throw it, you need big fingers, something I've always been blessed with. Actually, I started throwing the fork ball before I even knew what it was. In those backyard catch games with my brothers, I used to mess around with the pitch.

You hold the ball between the index and middle fingers, the ball shoved all the way back to the webbing between the two fingers. The ball should fit in there comfortably, although at first it won't. It takes a period of years to get your fingers molded that way. They must be able to have a very wide spread between them. My fingers have an abnormal split now, just because of this pitch.

I use the fork ball as my change-up. It came about almost by accident. I had tried every kind of change-up imaginable and nothing seemed to be working. Then, one day in San Diego, I was throwing between starts to Bob Barton, then a catcher with the Reds.

157

I started messing around with the fork ball, just as I had as a kid. The ball was jumping all over the place.

"Have you tried that in a game?" he asked. I told him no.

"You ought to try it," he said. "It's a great pitch. It's really off speed and it's moving like crazy."

So I tried it and each game it kept getting better and better. It is now one of my major pitches.

The fork ball comes to the plate slowly and with little rotation on it. Usually it will break straight down just as it gets to the plate, but sometimes it might jump right or left.

It is much like the knuckleball, another freak pitch.

THE KNUCKLEBALL AND OTHER FREAKS

The knuckleball is the most difficult of the freak pitches to control and is, therefore, the toughest for any pitcher to use. But it is also one of the best, the pitch that has made the likes of Phil Niekro and Wilbur Wood.

The pitcher doesn't know which way the pitch will break. It can rise, sink, jump to the left, to the right. If the pitcher doesn't know, how in the world is the batter going to know? It is a hard pitch to throw, a hard pitch to catch, and a hard pitch to hit.

There really isn't any correct way to throw the pitch. Most people, however, dig the fingernails of their index and middle fingers into the ball, then push it toward the plate without any strain on the arm. Others will fold their fingers over and really press their knuckles into the ball.

The only way to tell what is right for you is to watch the action of the ball. If it doesn't spin as it moves toward the plate, and if the catcher is having trouble handling it while it is going for strikes, you have yourself a good pitch.

Of all pitches, the screwball is the hardest on the arm, because it is unnatural. It is what you would call a reverse curve.

The pitch is gripped in a way that is the exact opposite of a curve ball, the index finger over the biggest seam. As you throw it, you turn your wrist, your elbow, and your forearm toward first base (if you are right-handed; toward third if you are left-handed).

You can see the tremendous stress put on the arm by this pitch, which is now the favorite of Mike Marshall and Jim Brewer. The greatest screwball pitcher of all time was probably Carl Hubbell, a Hall of Famer with the old New York Giants. The pitch took its toll on him. When he lets his pitching arm hang at his side, the palm of the hand is facing away from his body. That's what throwing so many screwballs can do to you.

The sinker is another effective pitch. Some guys have natural sinkers. Others have to work on it. What it really is is a fast ball. You grip it like a fast ball, with the thumb directly under the ball. You throw it with your hand slightly turned, less than with a slider, and you pull back on the laces, to give it backspin and cause it to sink.

It is an excellent pitch when you are looking for a ground ball to start a double play.

CONTROL

Being able to throw all the pitches is just one part of pitching. There is something else, just as important. You must be able to throw the pitches where you want them and with something on them. That is control.

A lot of people think control is just being able to throw strikes. Not so. You not only have to throw strikes in baseball, you have to throw pitches within the strike zone that the hitter can't hit.

Control is mostly a natural thing, but it is something that can be worked on and improved. And, let me tell you, there is no substitute for control. If you don't throw hard, you might be able to come up with a knuckleball or a vicious curve. But if you can't throw pitches to spots, you can't pitch.

You have to be able to throw the ball to the corners. You have to be able to throw it high or low. If you can do that with something on the ball—make your pitches when you need them—you'll be a winner.

The big word in control is concentration. Making the arm throw the ball where the brain says it should go and where the eyes see.

As he stands on the mound and takes the sign, the first thing that runs through a pitcher's mind is where he is going to throw the pitch. If a fast ball is called for and the hitter is known as a high fast ball hitter, the pitcher will try to throw a low fast ball. That is pitching. Throwing to the hitter's weakness and staying away from his strength.

As soon as he's made up his mind where he is going to throw the ball, he puts his eye right on that target and does nothing but concentrate on that spot.

A big mistake many pitchers make is to throw to the hitter instead of the catcher. Your target is the catcher, not the hitter. Say you want to throw a pitch low and outside. You look not at the hitter's knees in an effort to keep the ball down. Look at the catcher's knee that represents the area in which you want to throw the ball. If you want to throw up and in, look at the catcher's shoulder nearest the hitter.

Always pick something out to throw at and then hit that spot. This is pitching.

You must remember that you take one pitch and one hitter at a time. You have to know the situation of the game, to know the pitch you want to throw, to know where you want to throw it; then you block everything else out of your mind. Throw the pitch and then start all over again. It's a new situation.

You can help your control by having a purpose every time you throw a baseball. Whether in a game of catch or while pitching in a game. Always throw to a certain spot. If you miss the spot, try to figure out why.

PITCHING TO THE HITTER

Most clubhouse meetings that I've sat in on always go over a hitter this way. "Don't throw him a high fast ball. He kills that kind of pitch."

I kind of agree with Fred Norman, Cincinnati's little left-hander. He says he doesn't want to hear what a hitter can hit, he wants to hear what he can't hit.

It's a matter of positive thinking, something a pitcher must have if he is to succeed. Tell me how to get the hitter out. I don't want to be thinking out there about pitches I shouldn't throw. I want to think about the pitches I should throw.

True, by learning what a hitter can hit, you also learn what he can't hit. The idea is, though, that thinking about anything other than what you are trying to do is a distraction, and when pitching, you don't need any distractions.

I always start thinking about the upcoming game the night before. I go over the hitters in my mind and how I want to pitch them. I don't keep a "book," that is, a written history of what each man has done against me. But I know who has hurt me, when and on what pitch.

The trick is to know the hitters. You must always remember on the mound. Okay, so the last time I faced him, Jimmy Wynn of the Dodgers hit a home run off a high inside fast ball on a 2-and-0 pitch. How should I pitch him this time?

My first thought would be to make sure I don't fall behind in the count 2-and-0. This makes pitching tougher, especially to a power hitter who will sit and wait on the fast ball.

I would probably start him off with a fast ball, try to keep it down and on the outside corner. If I got that, I might come in with a slider in hopes he was looking for a pitch on the outside. If I was ahead in the count at 0-and-2, I might give him an inside fast ball. But I'd make certain the pitch was way inside— drive him back away. The trick is to be completely careful that you don't throw this pitch where he can hit it.

Now, with the count 1-and-2, I might try to nip the outside corner with a fast ball or drop a fork ball on him that is low and away, something really tough to hit.

All the time, as you work a hitter over, you are thinking of the situation in the game and your past experiences with a hitter.

While pitching, you actually have a partner. He is your catcher and it is he who calls the pitches. Before every game, you should sit down with him and go over the hitters, letting him know your thinking so that during the game, you and he can act as a unit, think as one.

When warming up before a game, it's good to have your regular catcher come down and catch you for a couple of minutes. That way, you get used to throwing to him and he gets used to handling your stuff.

The pitcher must never solely rely on the catcher to do his thinking. If the catcher signals for a pitch that you feel is wrong at that particular moment, shake him off by shaking your head. That tells him you want a different pitch.

Sometimes he may signal for the same pitch again. Shake him off again or call him out to the mound and discuss the situation. He may be able to convince you that he is right and that you should throw the pitch called for. In the end, though, it is the pitcher who must throw the ball and he must take the responsibility for the pitch.

A GAME OF CAT AND MOUSE

The battle between the pitcher and hitter is as much a battle of wits and nerves as it is a physical battle. Hitting, you see, is based on timing and concentration. If the pitcher can disrupt either, he has a big advantage.

Remember, the hitter will be thinking just as you are. What did he get me out with the last time? What did I hit off him last time? What's working for him today? Knowing this, the pitcher's thinking becomes doubly important. He not only must try to figure out what the hitter has done against him before, but what he is looking for this time.

All the while, you will be doing things to disrupt the hitter. You might shake off a sign just for the sake of appearance, to make him stand there for a while. Maybe you get ready, then step off the rubber and adjust your pants. When you started winding up, just to confuse his timing, you might double pump, bring the arms up over the head, bring them back down, and start the windup all over, doing it all in one motion. The trouble with this is, it's likely to throw your timing off, so don't overdo it.

If you really want to disrupt the hitter's train of thought, brush him back. Always, when throwing a brush-back pitch, remember that there is a danger involved. Be careful with it.

Throw the ball at the batter's body, just close enough to move him back off the plate. Use it when you have a batter crowding the plate or digging in.

Never intentionally throw at a hitter's head. This is called a beanball. It is illegal and can seriously hurt someone.

PITCHING FROM A STRETCH

No matter how good a pitcher you are, somebody is going to get on base against you. And when there is a runner on first or second you will work from the stretch position.

The object of pitching from the stretch is to keep the runners as close as possible to the base.

I start the stretch motion by placing my left foot—right foot for right-handers—up against the front of the rubber. My body is facing first base, the ball is in my glove, and I look in to take the sign.

Now I bring my hands up and together, meeting just about at the letters on the uniform. I stand straight, drop the hands to the belt and stop them. That is the set position and I can do two things from it. I can throw to a base in a pick-off attempt, or I can throw the pitch. I must, however, stop in the set position for a full second.

If I'm going to throw to the plate, after having looked at the runner on base, I try to make the motion as quickly as possible to cut down on the break a potential base stealer may get.

I don't bring my arms back over my head. My kick is somewhat toward first base, just to confuse the runner, then quickly toward home plate. I still reach back and push off the rubber, trying to throw just as hard as if I had taken my full windup.

The throw to first base is done quickly and the pitcher must step directly toward the base. Sometimes you will throw over there just to let the runner know that you're alive and well. Other times, when you use the quick snap throw, you will be trying to nail the man.

A right-hander has a more difficult problem, since his back is toward first base. He can't fake to the base because that's a balk, and the runner is awarded second base. He can't fake home and then throw to the base because that, too, is a balk.

The right-hander will take a quick pivot on the foot against the rubber—he might even step back off the rubber before trying the pick-off move—wheel with his left leg and throw to first as quickly

FROM THE STRETCH. Pitching from the stretch is somewhat different from a full windup. You take the sign, back foot on the rubber. When you come to the full stop, you check the runner, as I do here. This time the runner is at second base. In this sequence I have started to come to the plate before my head gets back around, being satisfied the runner wasn't going anywhere. Now you swing into the pitch, the kick not as high as on the full windup. Again with your eyes on the target, throw and completely follow through. (Photos by Fred Straub)

and accurately as possible. You must step toward the base before throwing, remember. Don't get too tricky. The idea is to keep the man close, not necessarily pick him off.

When looking at the runner, you must hold the ball long enough to make sure he stops. A walking lead—where the runner keeps edging off toward second base—is the most dangerous to the pitcher. It gives the runner an almost running start.

If the runner has too long a lead, throw over or step off the rubber. Sometimes look over at the base, look to the plate, then look

back again. You might catch him leaning toward second. Other times, look over and start for the plate as soon as you are sure the runner isn't going anywhere.

With a runner on second base, I normally stop for just a second or two longer than with a man at first. You want to make sure the runner stays close and you have your shortstop and second baseman faking in behind the runner. Stopping a bit longer gives them a chance to make the fake and still be in position to field the ball.

The pick-off at second comes off a sign from either the shortstop, second baseman, or catcher. It is something that must be practiced often, because it depends on timing.

Often you will go on a count. From the moment you look toward the plate, you will count to three and, on three, step back off the rubber, pivot all the way around and throw to the shortstop or second baseman, whichever was designated to cover.

The main thing is to get the back foot off the rubber, pivot quickly, and have the timing down to perfection.

FIELDING

A pitcher can really help himself if, in addition to being able to pitch well, he can field his position. And the play the pitcher will have to make most is on the bunt.

The best defense against the bunt, of course, is to make the batter pop the ball up. You will try to do this in bunt situations with fast balls, high and inside. However, the hitter usually has worked hard on his bunting and will often get the bunt down.

In a sacrifice bunt situation—the sacrifice being used to advance a runner without the bunter worrying about whether he is safe or not—the pitcher will break directly toward the plate. He must cover the middle area, the third baseman and first baseman taking the bunts to the right or left.

The pitcher, should he field the ball, will be listening to directions shouted out by the catcher. If the catcher shouts for a throw to second base, the pitcher will wheel and, without hesitation, throw there. If he yells first base, the pitcher will field the ball, turn and throw to first.

On the squeeze play, the pitcher should first think of making the batter miss the ball. If a right-hander is batting with a man at third and squares around to bunt, the ball will be thrown right at him. Drive him back out of there.

If a left-handed hitter is up, it becomes an automatic pitchout if the squeeze is on. You don't want him to be able to bunt the ball.

If the ball is bunted, the pitcher charges quickly just in case it is popped up. If it is on the ground, there will be virtually no chance for a play at the plate, the runner having broken on the pitch. Take a quick look to see, and if you think you can get the man, flip the ball home. Usually it will be an underhand toss, as you are coming in that direction anyway and won't have more than 25 feet or so to throw. If there is not a chance, chalk it up as a run against you and get the man at first.

The pitcher has a fielding responsibility on base hits, too. Don't just stand on the mound. Go somewhere and back up a base. If no one is on base, back up the throw to second on a single. If there's a man on first, immediately break to back up third base. If there's a man on second, your position is backing up the plate.

The pitcher also has a responsibility on infield pop-ups. He becomes the man in charge. He shouts out the name of the infielder who should catch the ball. This sounds easy, but sometimes it leads to confusion.

We had just obtained John Vukovich, a third baseman, from Milwaukee, when Clay Kirby had this happen to him. A pop was lofted between third and home. Johnny Bench got under the ball and Kirby was shouting, "John, John."

Hearing this, Vukovich came in, collided with Bench, and the ball fell. Kirby completely forgot that his catcher and his new third baseman have the same name.

chapter fourteen

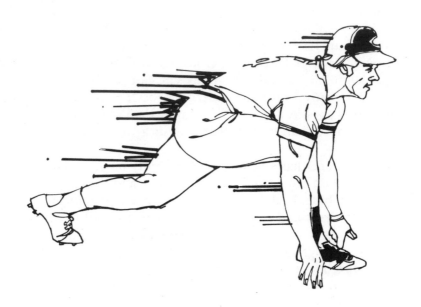

The instructions on how to play winning baseball are now yours. What you must do now is put them to use—and the only way to do that is to get yourself your glove, your bat, and your ball—and go out and practice.

The most important thing you will do as a baseball player is practice. It is fun to play the game, but only if you play it well, and the only way you will play it well is to practice.

Organized teams such as Little League, American Legion, high school, and the like will have coaches running the show.

When going out on your own, always make sure that there's a purpose in what you're doing. When playing ball with a friend, work on your skills. Make your throws count. If throwing from the outfield, try to work on accuracy and building up your arm. If

168

practice makes perfect

batting, work on hitting to the other field or hitting the ball through the middle.

Find out what you can and can't do. Try to improve on the skills you find hardest to come by. If you have trouble going to your right after ground balls, have your friends hit you balls to your right.

ALWAYS WARM UP

I don't care if you're just going out in the park with your friends or if you're working out with your Little League team. The first thing you must do is loosen up properly.

That means do some running, a lap around the field or so, and

GETTING LOOSE. Here are a couple of exercises that a player should do before a game to loosen the muscles and stretch them out. The most important thing in pre-game exercising is to make sure the muscles are loose enough that you will avoid pulling them during the game. (Photos by Fred Straub)

some stretching exercises as explained earlier. Once you have finished doing this and have worked up a little sweat and loosened up the muscles, it is time to start throwing the ball.

Start slowly. Play catch with a teammate about 20 feet apart. As the muscles in the arm become looser and less sore—yes, when you start throwing, your muscles usually do feel a bit stiff and sore— move the distance back. You should throw for at least 10 minutes to make sure the arm is well heated. That way, when you have to make a quick, difficult throw, there is less chance of injuring an arm.

This is as good a time as any to talk about sore arms. Some guys have arms that can take anything. Pedro Borbon, Cincinnati's tireless relief pitcher, is one of those guys. The only time you see him in the training room is when he is borrowing a pair of scissors to cut one of his teammates' hair. He is also a barber, you see.

It is normal for the arm to become sore during the spring. This comes from using muscles that haven't been used in some time. Most of the time you can throw right through this kind of soreness. After two or three days, the muscles will be loose again and begin to regain their strength.

Sometimes, if you throw a great deal, the arm will become tired. It will actually feel heavy and you won't be able to get much zip on the ball. If it feels this way, slow down for a couple of days. Limit your throwing, because a tired arm can lead to a sore arm.

Nothing can be much worse than for a ball player to come up with a sore arm—the real thing, I mean. If you have a trainer and your arm is sore, go to him. Tell him where the pain is located and what kind of pain it is. There are many things he can do to help it.

If you don't have a trainer and it pains you to throw, you might have to see a doctor. Often the cause is a mild muscle strain. It is best, though, to have it checked out. It could be something that requires medical attention.

It's better to be cautious with arm trouble than to push it. A sore arm could end your baseball career before it begins.

I also believe in getting loose before you hit. This means make use of a lead bat if one is available. Swing it, not as hard as you swing in a game, but enough so that you exercise the muscles you will use in the swing. If there is no lead bat available, swing two bats at once.

JUMPING JACKS. It isn't always tough to exercise, as proved here during some jumping jack exercises at spring training. (Photo by Fred Straub)

This does two things. First, it loosens the muscles for you; second, it makes the bat you will use in a game seem lighter and easier to swing.

AFTER YOU'RE LOOSE

In an organized practice, you will usually begin working on situations and special skills after batting practice. Early in the year, you will work on bunt coverage, cutoff plays, plays in which the pitcher covers first, and backing up the bases.

The coach will put the players in their respective positions in the field, let some of the extra players run the bases, and set up plays. This should be done for 15 minutes or so every practice session before games begin, drilling each reaction to a situation into the players. Then, when it comes time for a relay in the outfield or a cutoff play, it will come naturally to the players.

AFTER THE FUNDAMENTALS

Once all this is taken care of, it is time for batting practice. With the Reds, we let the pitchers hit first. And I would strongly suggest that the pitchers also make sure they get their bunting practice in every day.

After the pitchers come the extra men, the reserves. They will hit as the regulars go to their positions and take ground balls or fly balls hit by coaches. When I moved to third base during the 1975 season, I saw to it that I took at least a half hour of ground balls a day at my new position.

Finally, the regulars take their turn in the batting cage. We normally break the regulars down into two groups of four, each group hitting for 20 minutes or so. You may start out taking 10 swings each, then seven, then five, then three. As time is running out, you will be trying to get every swing in you can.

As the regulars are hitting, the pitchers whose turn it is to throw on the sideline are doing that. They'll be throwing maybe 15 or 20 minutes a day between starts, working on pitches that have given them trouble or working on their control. They never should be throwing just to be throwing.

Also, while the regulars are hitting, the extra men are taking grounders or flies at their respective positions. What you are trying to avoid is having any period of time where men are just standing around doing nothing. The practice must always be moving.

AFTER BATTING PRACTICE

If you've practiced the way you're supposed to – and that is hard—

by now, you are tired. It's the perfect time to do your running.

On the day of a game, the regulars don't run. They have to be fresh for the game. The reserve players, however, do 10 to 12 sprints of 50 yards or so, sprinting down and jogging back.

The pitchers who aren't pitching that day will do about 15 sprints. The starting pitcher will relax in the clubhouse, if you are fortunate enough to have one.

On days when there is no game, everyone should run, even the superstars.

Remember, practice the game the way you are going to play the game. Practice hard and play hard. Run hard and, above all else, hustle every moment you're on the baseball field. That will make you a winning player.

glossary

ARTIFICIAL TURF: A man-made substance, such as Astro-Turf, to replace grass covering the playing area.

AT BAT: An official time to the plate.

BACKSTOP: The area of the playing field directly behind home plate that a pitch will hit if it gets past the catcher. Also a slang term for the catcher.

BACK UP: To rèinforce a player actually making the play in case the ball gets past him.

BAD BALL HITTER: A batter who regularly swings at pitches out of the strike zone.

BAG: Any base except home plate. Must be 15 inches square and from three to five inches thick.

BAIL OUT: See stepping in the bucket.

BALK: An illegal move made by the pitcher with a runner or runners on base, allowing them to advance one base.

BALL: A pitch ruled outside the strike zone by the umpire.

BASE HIT: A term indicating a single. A two-base hit is a double. A three-base hit is a triple.

BASE ON BALLS: Four pitched balls out of the strike zone, allowing the batter to go to first base. Also called a walk.

BAT: The wood tool the batter uses to hit the ball.

BAT SPEED: The speed with which the batter moves the bat in an effort to contact the ball.

BATTER'S BOX: The marked-off area to the right and left of the plate in which the batter must stand.

BATTING ORDER: Official listing of the order in which players come to bat.

BEANBALL: An illegal pitch thrown at the batter's head, intended either to hit him or to move him off the plate. When thrown at the body to move batter back, it is a Brush-back.

BLOOPER: A ball hit on a soft fly.

BREADBASKET CATCH: A catch of a high fly with the glove held at the waist.

BULLPEN: The area where relief pitchers warm up.

BUNT: Ball that is not swung at, but hit softly. The idea usually is to advance a runner.

CATCHER'S BOX: The area marked off behind the plate in which the catcher must stand. If outside the area, it is a catcher's balk and the batter is credited with a ball.

CATCHER'S SIGNAL: The hand code given the pitcher by the catcher to tell him to throw a certain pitch.

CHANGE-UP: A pitch that is slower than the pitcher normally throws. Also called a change of pace or letup.

CHOKE UP: To hold the bat up from the bottom of the bat.

CURVE: A pitch thrown by a right-hander that curves away from a right-handed batter or by a left-hander that curves away from a left-handed batter.

CUTOFF: To intercept a thrown ball, usually to prevent a hopeless play or keep a secondary runner from advancing.

CUTOFF MAN: The player who intercepts the throw.

DEAD BALL: A ball out of play.

DELIVERY: The act of pitching the ball.

DIAMOND: The entire playing field. Also a name for just the infield.

DOUBLE-HEADER: Two games played the same day.

DOUBLE PLAY: A play by the defense in which two offensive players are put out.

DOUBLE PUMP: A type of pitching motion in which the pitcher brings his arms up above his head twice before delivering. It is used to throw a batter's timing off.

DRAG BUNT: A bunt in which the ball is pushed or "dragged" past the pitcher toward the second baseman.

DUGOUT: The area of the field in which the players are seated during a game when they are not playing.

EARNED RUN: A run for which the pitcher will be held accountable—not a run scored because of an error.

EARNED RUN AVERAGE: A statistic compiled by multiplying the number of earned runs by nine, then dividing by innings pitched. It is a measure of a pitcher's effectiveness.

ERROR: A misplay that lets a runner reach or advance a base.

EXTRA-BASE HIT: A fair ball on which the batter makes more than one base.

FAIR BALL: A batted ball that is hit within the playing field's boundaries.

FLY: A ball hit in the air to the outfield.

FOLLOW-THROUGH: The motion of a pitcher after he has released the pitch.

FORCE OUT: A play in which a base runner is retired by a fielder who touches the base before the runner gets there, after the batter has forced the runner to make that base by becoming a base runner himself.

FORK BALL: A pitch held between two fingers, as if in a fork.

FOUL BALL: A ball landing outside the boundary lines of the playing field.

FOUL TIP: A ball that is batted directly into the catcher's hands or straight back.

FULL COUNT: Three balls and two strikes on a batter.

FULL WINDUP: The pitching motion used with no one on base.

FUNGO: A ball hit to a player during practice out of another player's or coach's hand, rather than from a pitch.

FUNGO BAT: A bat used to hit fungoes, usually longer and thinner than an ordinary bat.

GRAND SLAM: Home run with the bases full.

GROUND RULES: Those regulations relating to a specific ball park, designed to prevent any interference with normal play.

GUESS HITTER: A batter who looks for a certain pitch rather than just reacting to the ball.

HEAD-FIRST SLIDE: An effort to get to the base safely by throwing the body through the air, head first.

HIT AND RUN: A play in which the batter hits the pitch as the runner is going. He must swing at the ball no matter where it is pitched.

HIT BATTER: A legal batter struck with a pitched ball. He is awarded first base.

HOME RUN: A four-base hit.

HOOK SLIDE: A slide in which the runner comes into the base feet first, turning his body away from the fielding and hooking the base with his toe.

INFIELD: The area of the playing field occupied by the catcher, pitcher, shortstop, and basemen.

INFIELDER: Anyone who plays the infield.

INNING: The division of a baseball game in which each team gets three outs. There are nine innings in a regulation game.

JUMP: The break a runner gets as he tries to steal a base.

KNUCKLEBALL: A pitch held against the knuckles or with the fingernails, one that may break in any direction.

LACES: The threads that hold a ball together. Also referred to as the seam.

LEAD: The distance a runner gets away from the base.

LEADOFF MAN: The first batter in the official batting order.

LEFT ON BASE: A runner who doesn't score before three men are out.

LETTERS: The name of the team written across the chest of a uniform.

LINE DRIVE: Sharply hit ball that travels on a straight line.

LINEUP: Same as batting order.

MOUND: The rise in the ground, 10 inches, from where the pitcher pitches.

ON BASE: A runner on first, second, or third.

ON DECK: The player in the batting order who hits after the man at bat.

ONE-HOPPER: A ground ball that takes only one bounce before reaching the fielder.

OPPOSITE FIELD: The area of the field to which a batter is not expected to be able to hit: right field for a right-handed hitter and left field for a left-handed hitter.

OUTFIELD: The area of the field that is beyond the infield; left, center, and right field.

PALM BALL: A pitch thrown with the palm of the hand, used as a change-up.

PASSED BALL: A pitch that gets past the catcher that the catcher should have handled.

PEPPER GAME: Practice before a game for warming up, a batter repeatedly hitting the ball to at least one fielder.

PICK-OFF: An attempt to catch a runner off base.

PINCII HITTER: A batter who substitutes for the scheduled hitter.

PINCH RUNNER: A base runner who substitutes for a player already occupying a base.

PINE TAR: A sticky substance applied to the bat to give a better grip.

PITCHING ROTATION: The order in which a team's pitching staff starts games.

PITCHING STAFF: The entire number of pitchers on a team.

PITCHOUT: A ball deliberately delivered wide so that the batter can't reach it. Used to break up attempted hit-and-run or steal.

POP FLY: A short, high fly that can be caught easily.

POWER HITTER: A man who is capable of hitting home runs.

PULL HITTER: A batter who hits mostly to his power field: right for a left-hander, left for a right-hander.

RELAY MAN: A player who intercepts a throw and throws it to another player in an effort to retire a runner.

RELIEF PITCHER: A pitcher who comes into a game to replace another.

RESIN BAG: A bag of resin used to help the pitcher grip the ball.

ROOKIE: A first-year player.

RUN BATTED IN: A statistic that credits a man for hitting a ball that scored a run.

RUNDOWN: A play in which a runner is caught between bases.

SACRIFICE: A bunt whose purpose is to advance a runner at the expense of the batter being put out.

SACRIFICE FLY: An outfield fly that scores a runner from third base.

SAFETY SQUEEZE: A bunt in which a runner on third base waits to see if the ball is successfully bunted before trying to score.

SAVE: A statistic credited a relief pitcher who enters a game with his team in front and preserves the lead.

SCREWBALL: A pitch that, when thrown by a right-hander, curves in on a right-handed batter and does the opposite when thrown by a left-handed pitcher.

SHUTOUT: A game in which one team does not score.

SIDEARM: A pitching motion in which the pitcher throws from the side.

SIGNALS: Signs, usually in a manual code, to tell a player what play is being used.

SINGLE: A fair hit good for one base.

SINGLES HITTER: A batter who usually hits for no more than one base.

SLIDE: A means of reaching base by propelling the body across the ground.

SLIDER: A pitch that looks like a fast ball but that breaks quickly and late, sliding six inches or so.

SLUMP: A period of time when a batter has trouble hitting safely or when a pitcher has trouble winning.

SPITBALL: An illegal pitch in which saliva is added to the ball to make it break.

SQUEEZE: A play in which a batter tries to bring a runner home from third by bunting.

STEAL: To advance a base without the assistance of the ball being hit or the umpire awarding him that base. The base runner tries to steal while the pitcher is pitching.

STEPPING IN THE BUCKET: A slang term for a batter who steps away from the plate when hitting. Also called bailing out.

STRETCH POSITION: The motion a pitcher uses with men on base. It is a two-part motion, interrupted by a pause in the middle. The halt keeps base runners from running to the next base while pitching.

STRIKE: A pitch within the strike zone that isn't swung at or a pitch that is swung at and missed. Also a foul ball not caught by a fielder.

STRIKEOUT: The batter is retired on three strikes.

STRIKE ZONE: The area over the plate between the batter's knees and armpits.

SUICIDE SQUEEZE: A bunt play in which the runner from third breaks as the ball is pitched. The batter tries to bunt the ball. If he misses the ball, the runner is almost certain to be put out.

SWING: An attempt to hit the ball with the bat.

SWITCH-HITTER: A batter who can hit both left- and right-handed.

TAG: A situation in which a runner is touched with the ball while not occupying a base and is called out.

TAGGING UP: Re-touching a base on a fly ball, something a base runner must do if he hopes to advance after the catch.

TAKE: Let a pitch go by.

TAKE OUT: To slide into a fielder to keep him from throwing the ball.

TRAP: To catch a ball the moment it leaves the ground on the bounce instead of on a fly. This is called short-hopping the ball.

TRIPLE: A hit on which the batter gets three bases.

TRIPLE PLAY: A play in which three men are put out.

UMPIRE: A judge designated to make sure a game is run by the rules and who makes all judgments in the game.

UNIFORM: The official costume worn by a team.

UTILITY PLAYER: A reserve who is versatile and can be used in any of several positions.

WASTE PITCH: A pitch thrown intentionally off the plate so the batter won't swing at it.

WILD PITCH: A pitch so wild that it can't be handled by the catcher, allowing a runner to advance.

WINNING PITCHER: Pitcher credited in scoring with game won. A starting pitcher must pitch five or more innings and leave with his team leading, the team retaining the lead. A relief pitcher gets a win when his team takes the lead while he is pitching.

index